BEAUTIFUL BLUE & YOU... TOO

By

Michael Richardson and

Dr. Melinda Lincoln-Richardson

Copyright © 2023 by Michael Richardson and
Dr. Melinda Lincoln-Richardson-All Rights Reserved.

It is not legal to reproduce, duplicate, or transmit any part of this document in either electronic means or printed format. Recording of this publication is strictly prohibited.

Dedication

We dedicate our second book, BEAUTIFUL BLUE & YOU . . . TOO, to those who appreciate the beauty of nature. To persons who see the wonders of the world daily and who feel the tranquility of the water, this book is devoted to you.

Separate, but never apart, we become one with nature. Our growth takes place continually, much like the evolution of our natural surroundings. We not only see newness taking shape with the seasons, but we feel the changes that will enhance our growth and development throughout the years.

Together, surrounded by the splendor of nature, we learn to face daily challenges and difficult obstacles. The need to make every effort to do our best, propels us forward to survive. We become empowered with our own values and beliefs.

Just like the magnificence of "Beautiful Blue", become resilient. As the wind blows, change your direction to achieve success. Always strive for a better tomorrow.

Preface

BEAUTIFUL BLUE & YOU . . . TOO, captures the most unique moments to uplift your spirit. New levels of awareness will appear through your appreciation of nature. We hope your senses will take flight as you explore new dimensions of understanding life through nature's image. Whether "Beautiful Blue" climbs rocks, dives for sustenance, ascends through the air, or lands flawlessly on a moment's notice, we learn priceless life lessons applied to our personal path, as well.

The extraordinary photos capture rare instances of solitude, determination, exploration, and inspiration. Look for Blue's strength and resilience and apply these assets to your own existence. We are surrounded by these beautiful gifts of nature daily. They will motivate us to apply nature's lessons to our best future.

With each narration shadowing every photo, "Beautiful Blue" becomes personified with a profound voice. He speaks directly to you sharing his thoughts, ideas, and concerns, as he traverses through life. Navigating best personal decisions to thrive, "Beautiful Blue" reminds the reader that life empowers us with responsibilities, promises, and obligations. Find the right path and make the best life choices to succeed. Fulfilling one's life goals is a gift leading to a treasured existence. We hope you enjoy BEAUTIFUL BLUE & YOU . . . TOO, and find an enhanced you at the end of this beautiful journey.

Cheers,

Michael and Melinda

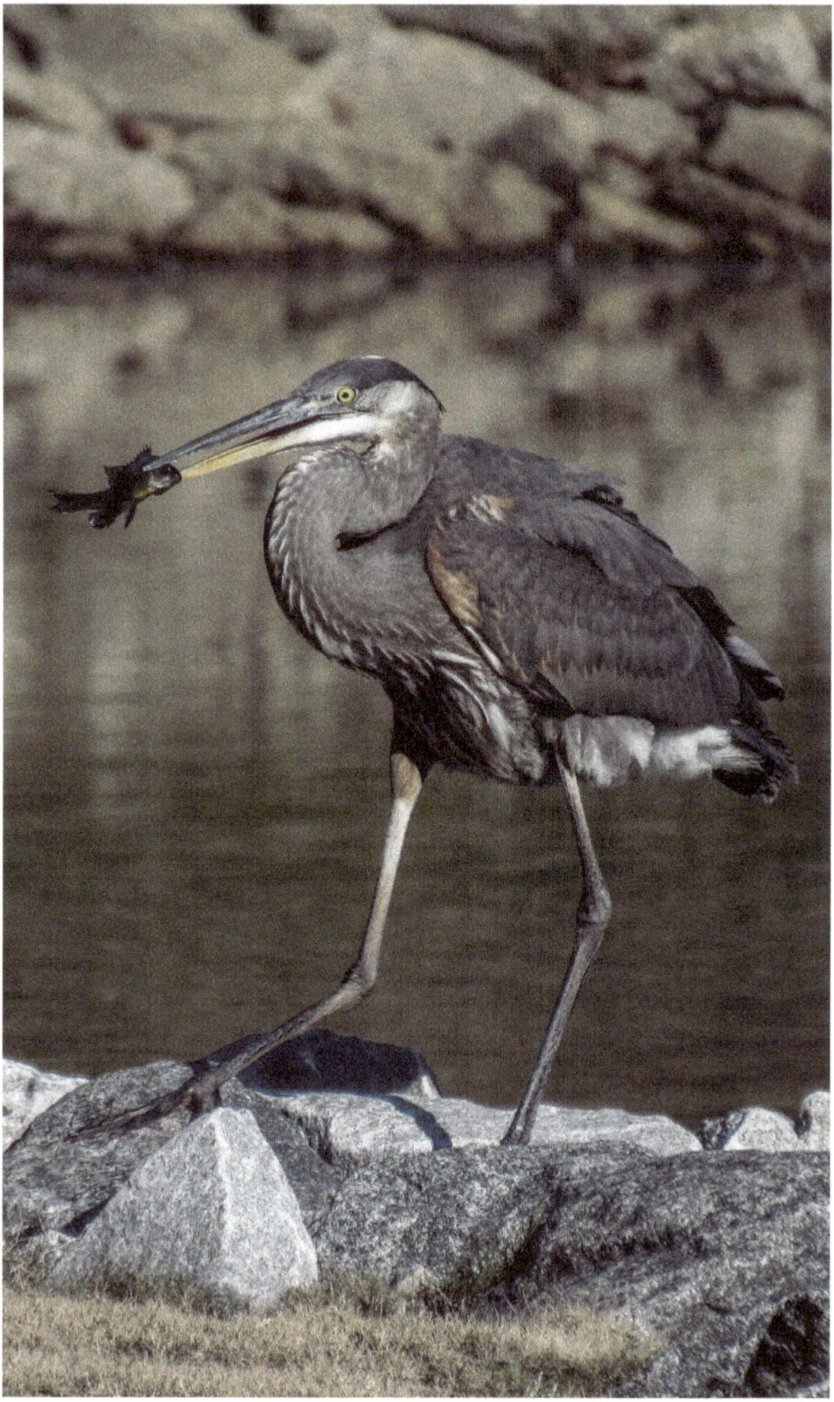

Morning Mate... Back to reconnect with life. A closer look at the world from inside out and deep within our being. Our next adventure awaits.

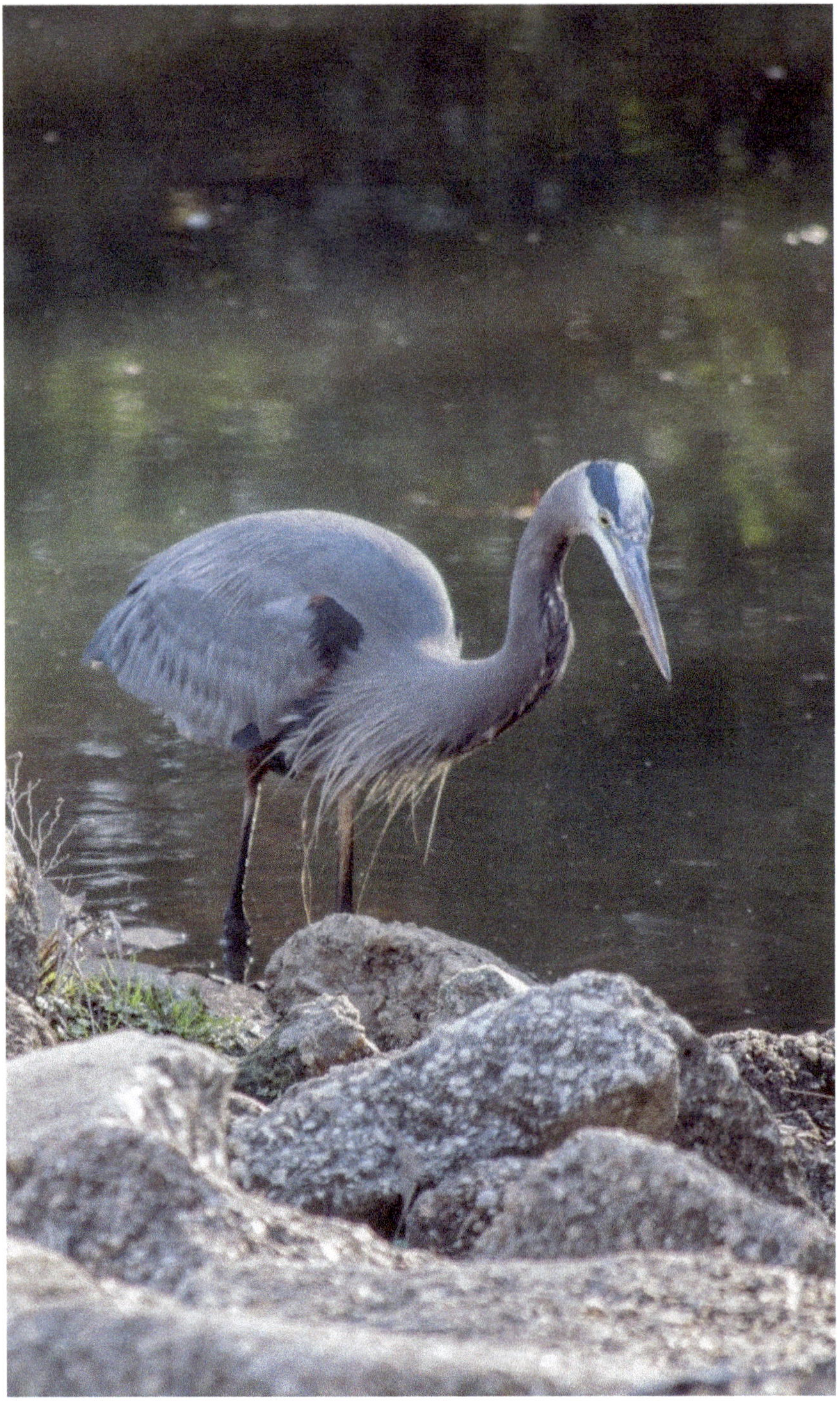

Monitor each motion with introspection and thought. Hesitation is never an option. Share kindness and joy with all.

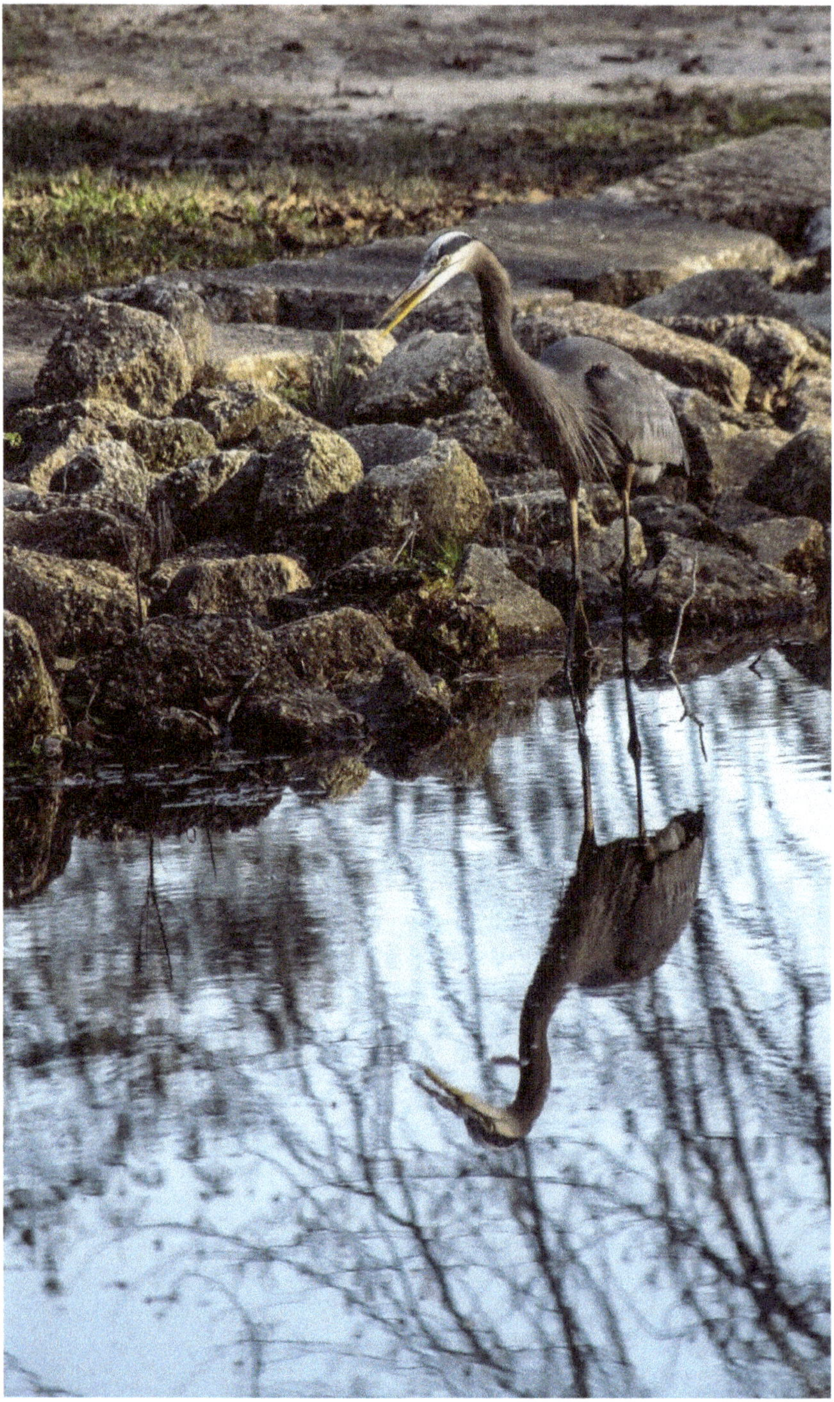

Images are truly remarkable. Unique and inspired by natural beauty. Anything can be achieved.

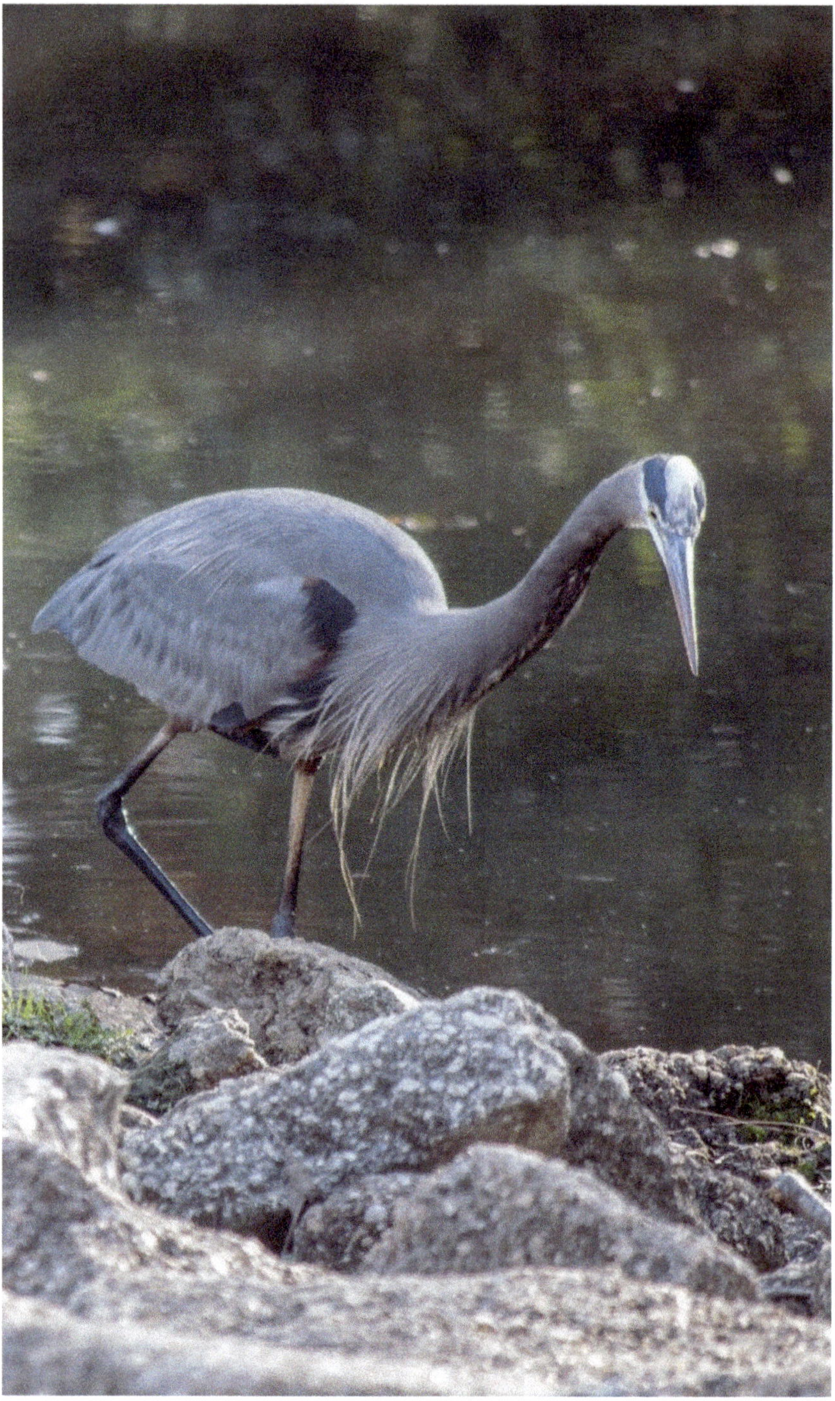

New experiences await. Eagerness for the unknown cradles us with anticipation and hope. Create your destiny with each step.

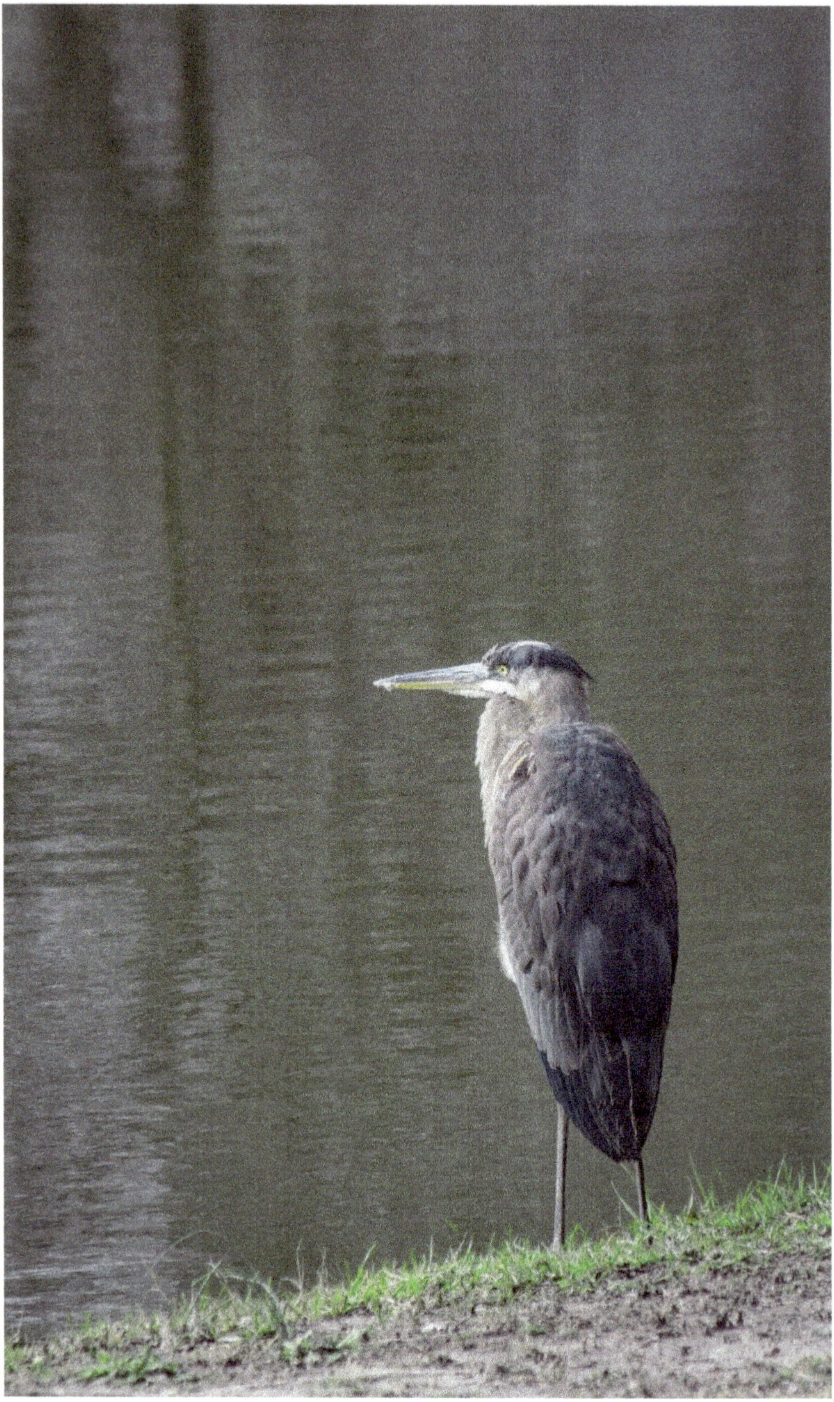

Contemplative by nature. Be steadfast in your commitment to life. Live fully and sleep well.

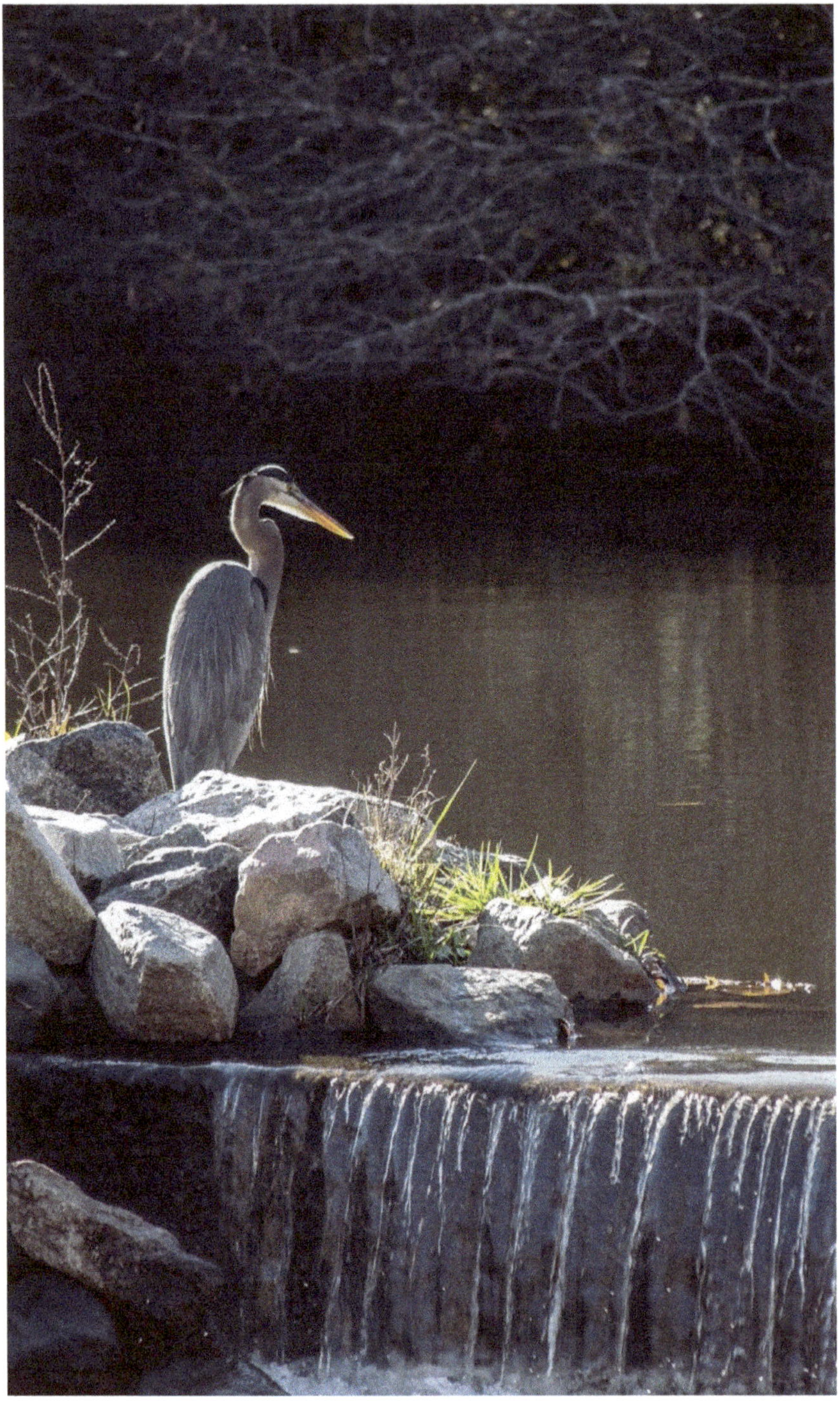

No one knows our secrets, but they will be revealed in time. Recognize who you are and the rest will fall into place naturally. Stand tall.

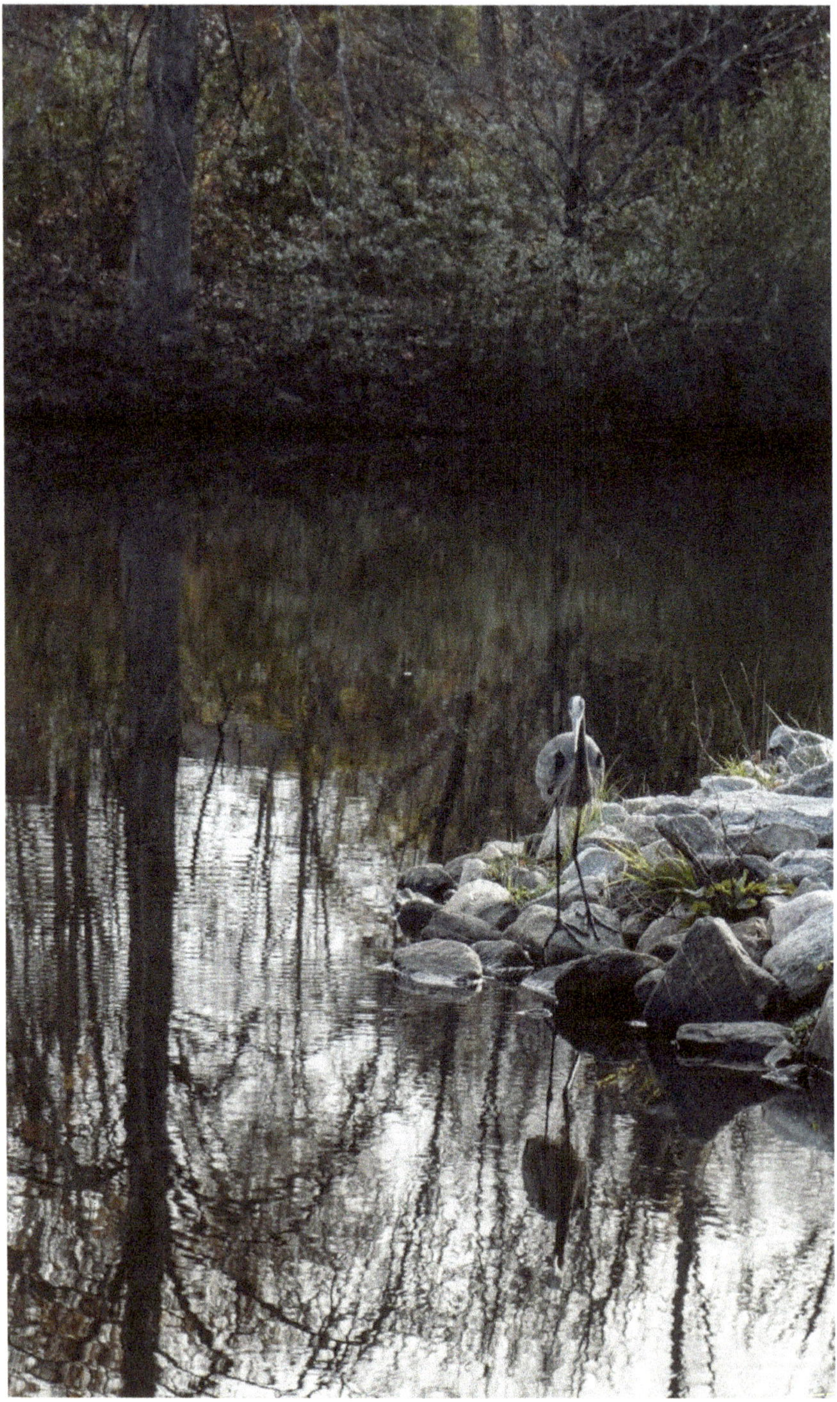

Reflective in thought. Find your direction and meet unwavering goals. Upon consideration, wishes do come true.

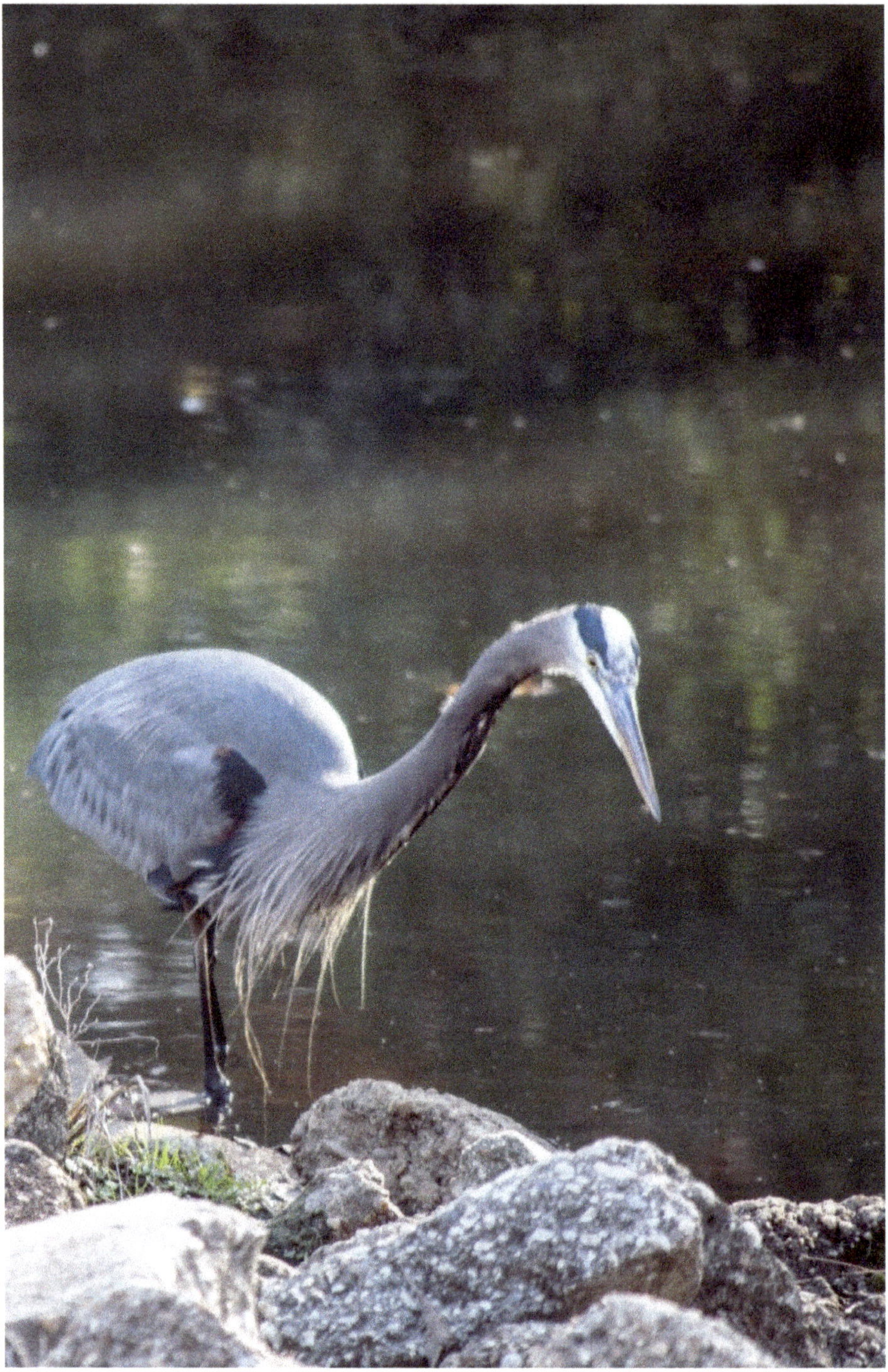

Sometimes, we change direction and alter our course.

Rely on instinct. Steady, but ready...

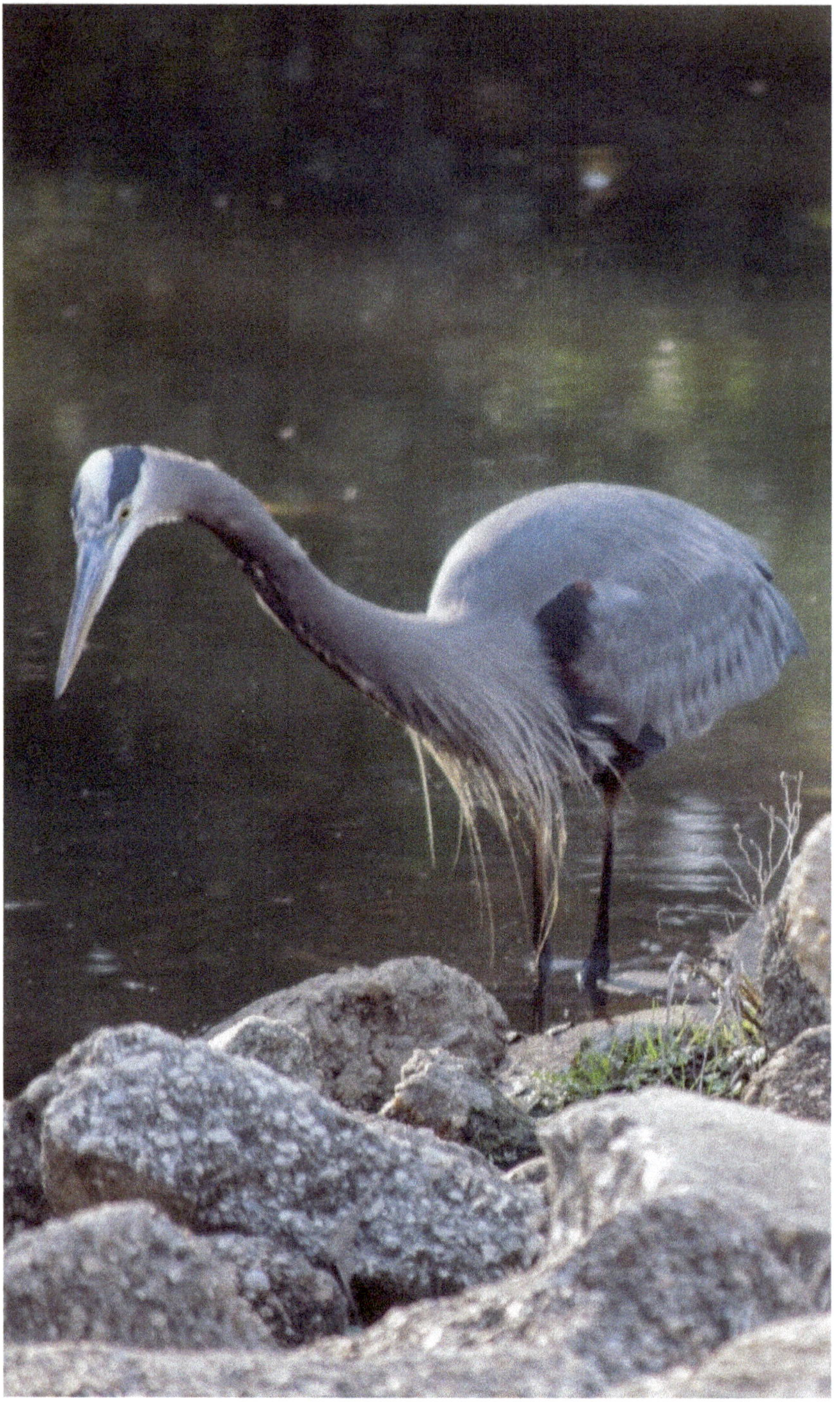

Vibrant blue steps provide a path of confidence and intrigue. Beauty is abundant and provides resilience within our being.

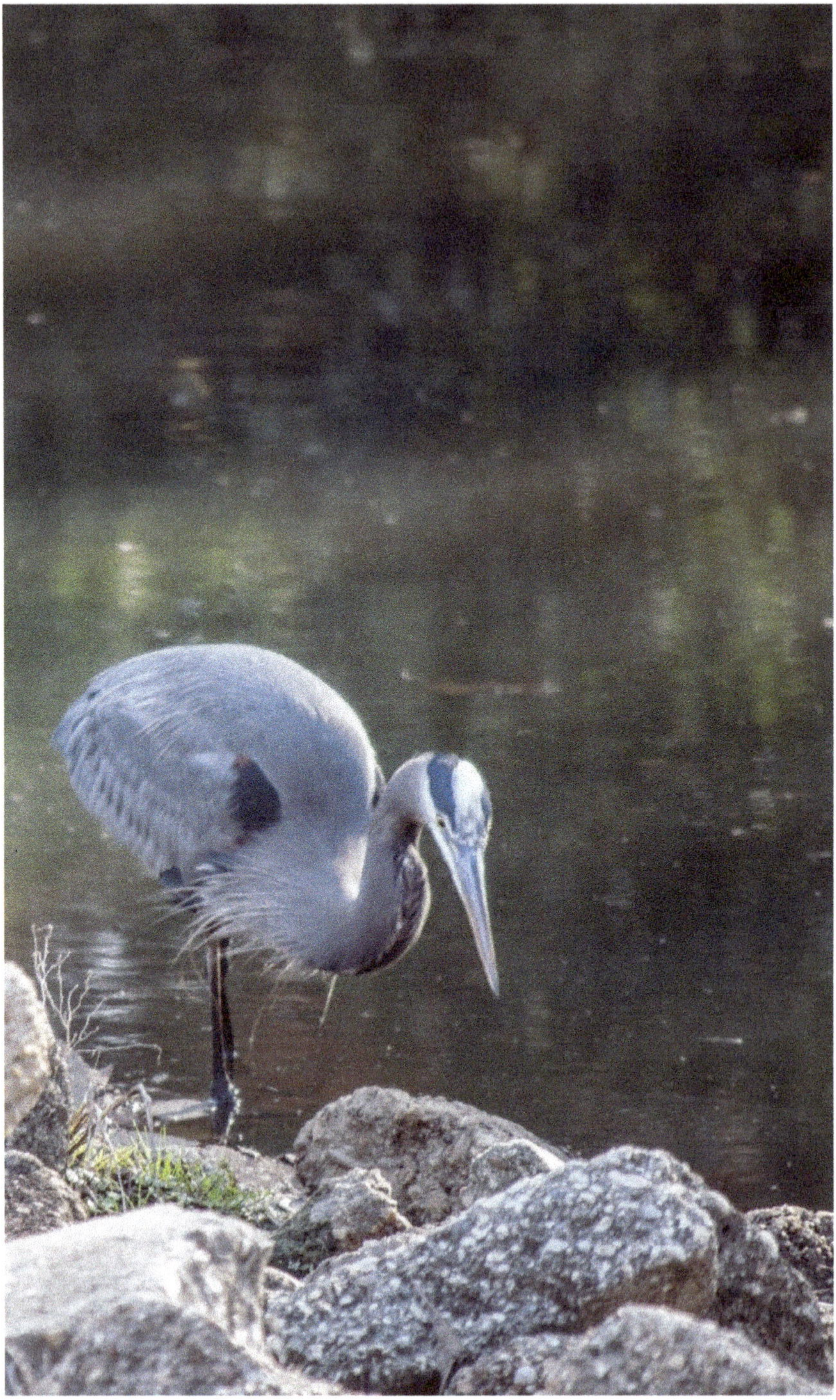

Breakfast looks tempting. Start the day with hope as you step forward to tomorrow. Each thought inspires the best within.

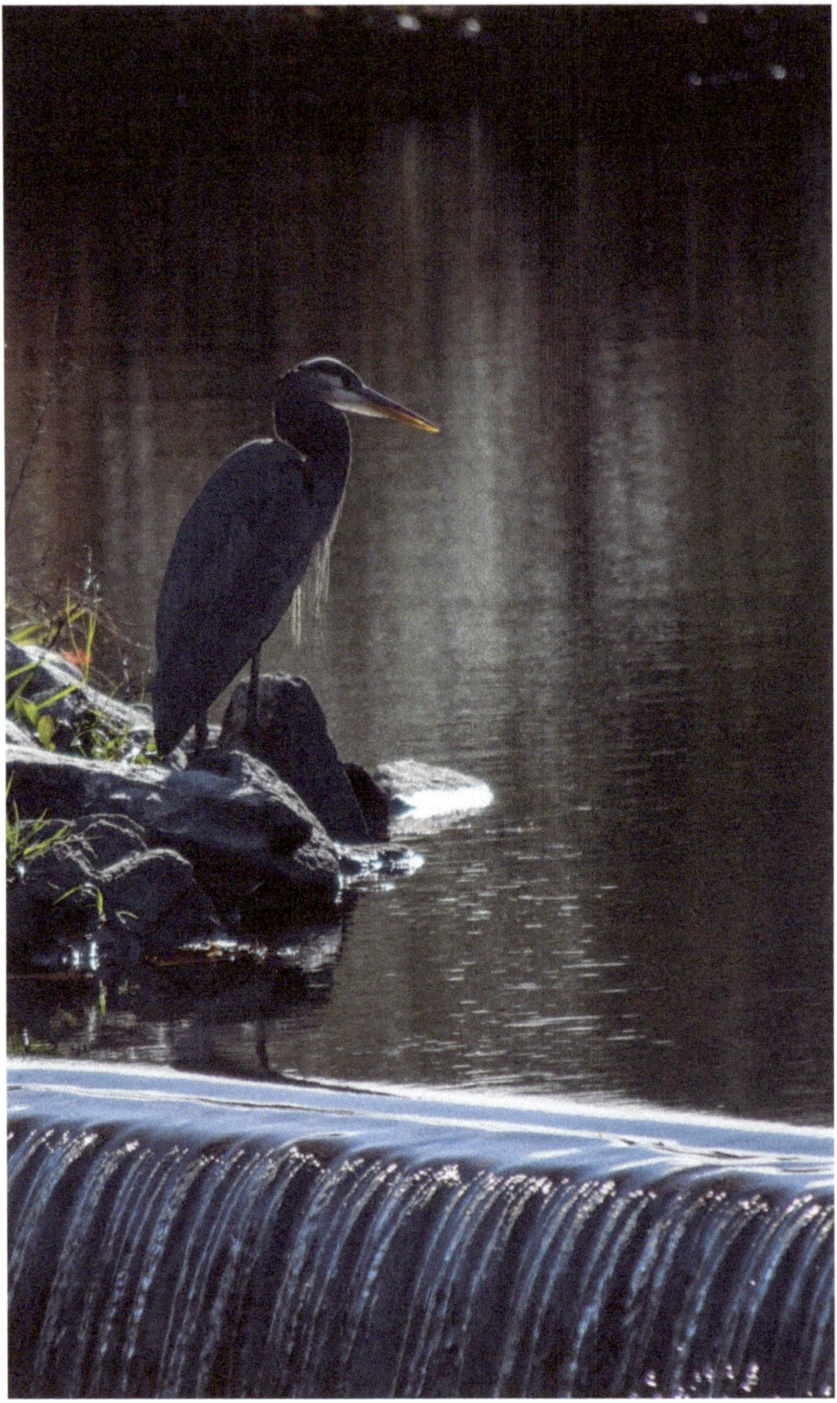

Beautiful Blue enhances the color of nature. Reality is a sheer glimmer of truth and beauty, everlasting.

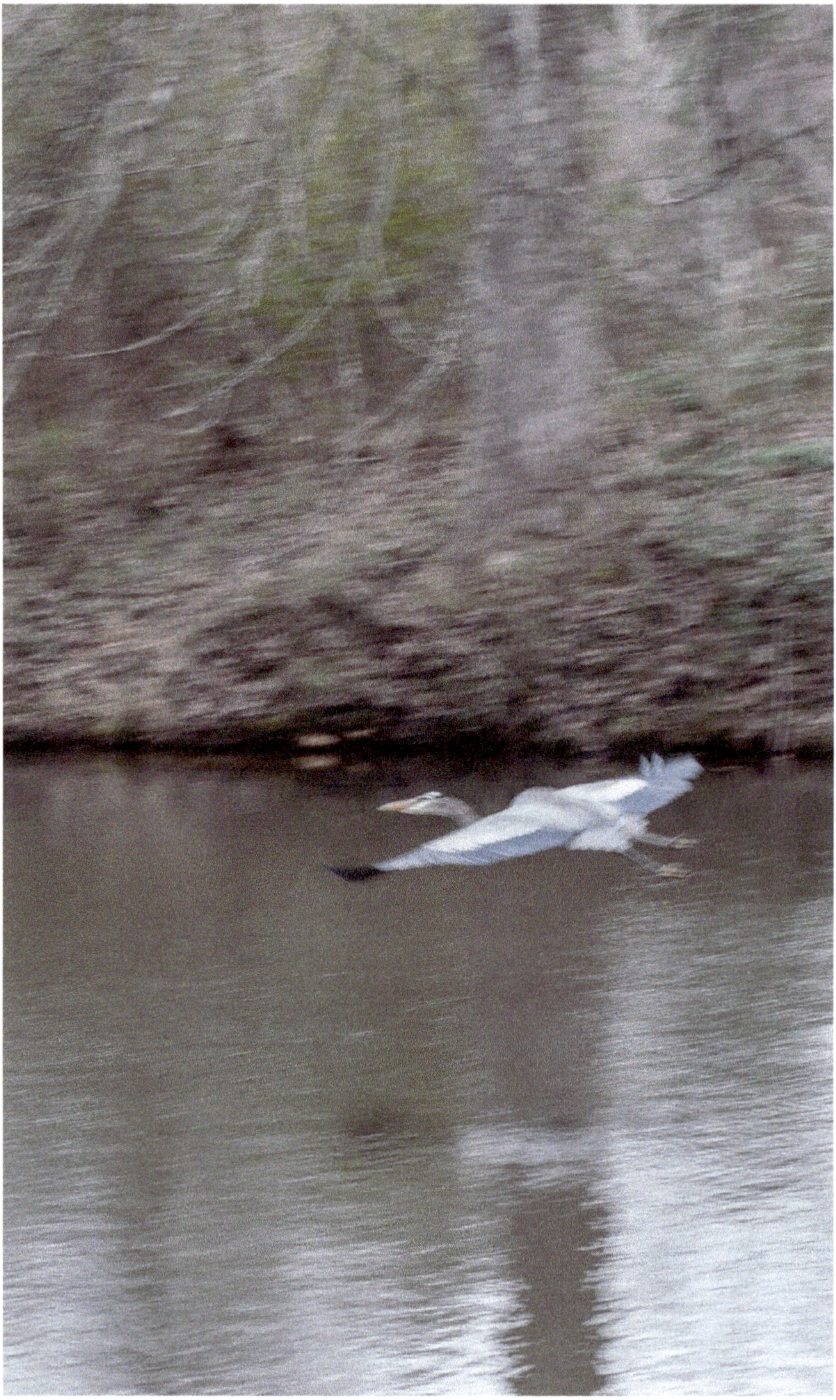

Gliding through life is a reward well earned. Enjoy the moment. Fill your soul with freedom and cherish your new empowerment to be your best.

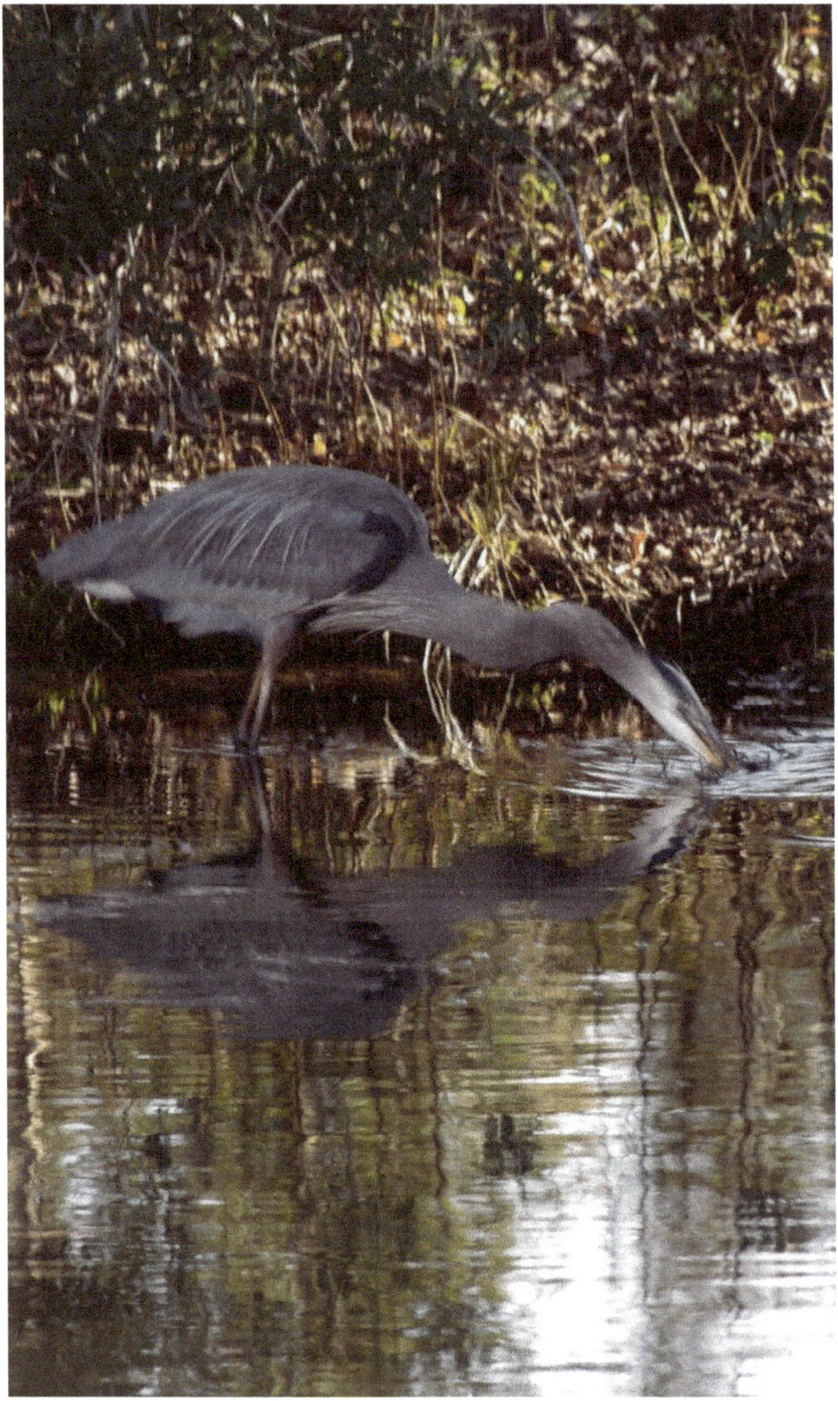

Begin with the nearest reality and make it greater. Join expectations with what can be a bountiful day for all.

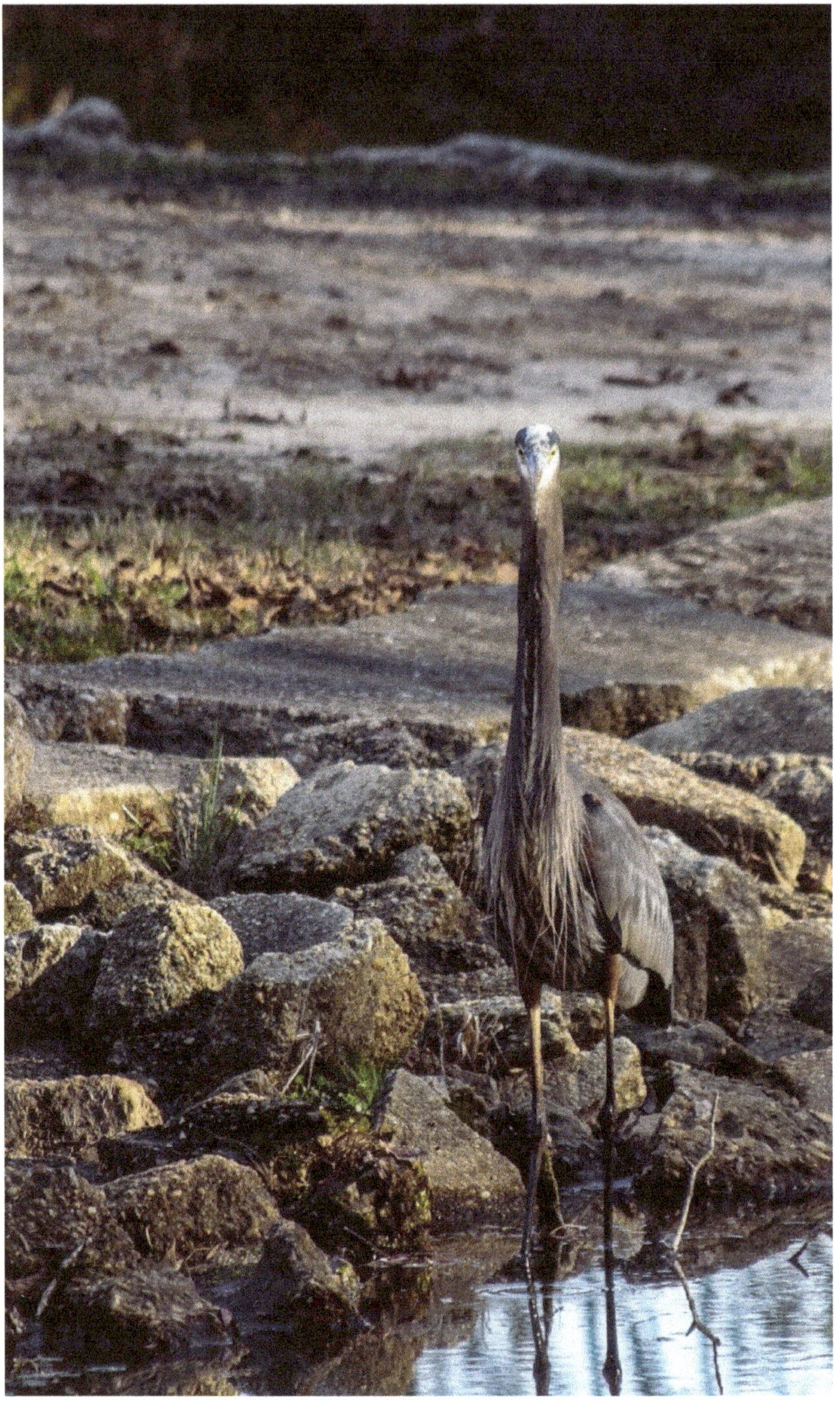

Ask one simple question... Are you ready to live and enjoy life fully, without questioning life's limits? Just be yourself for astounding results.

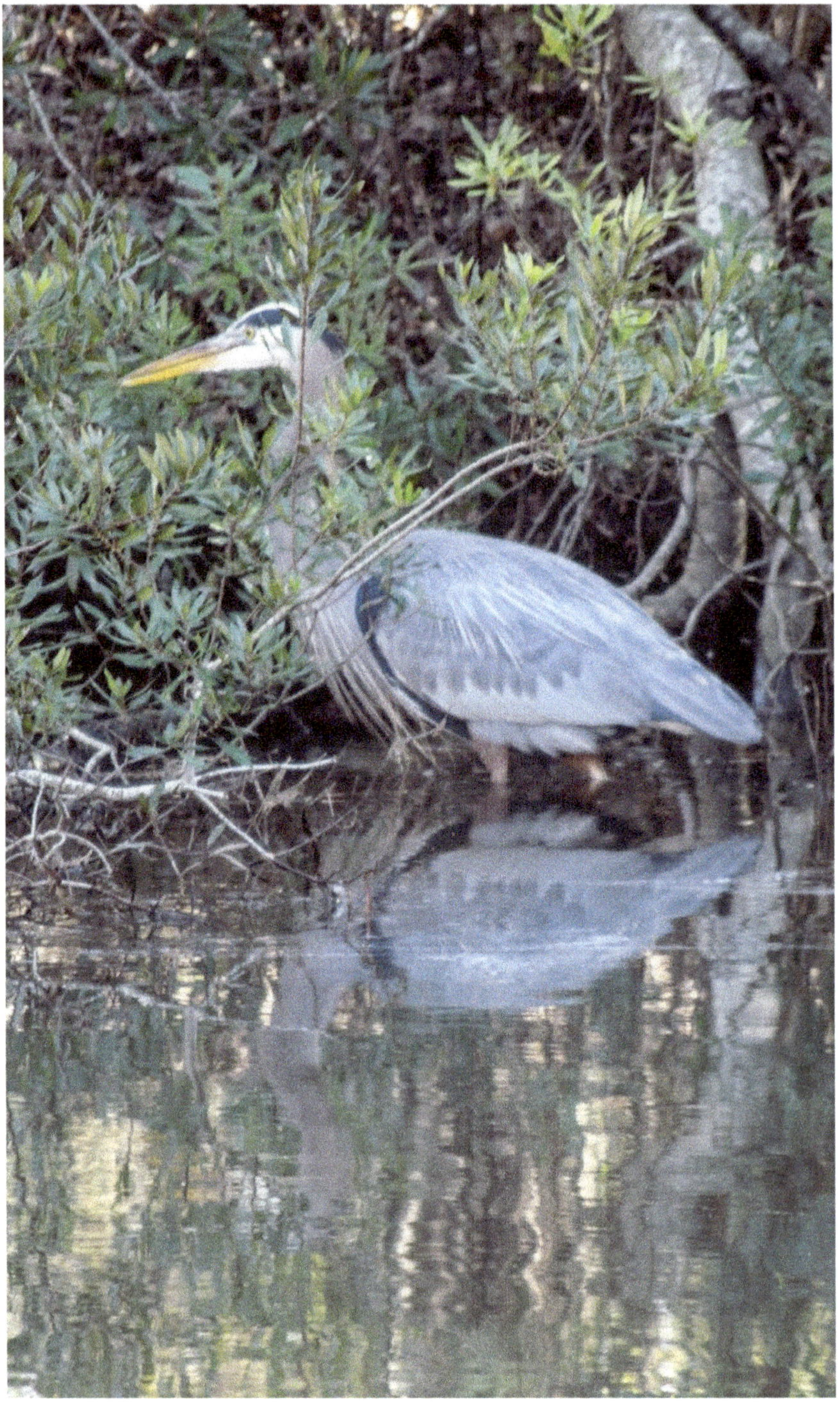

It is our reflective nature to view life fully. With each moment comes a new realization to build upon the past, acknowledge the present, and make it greater.

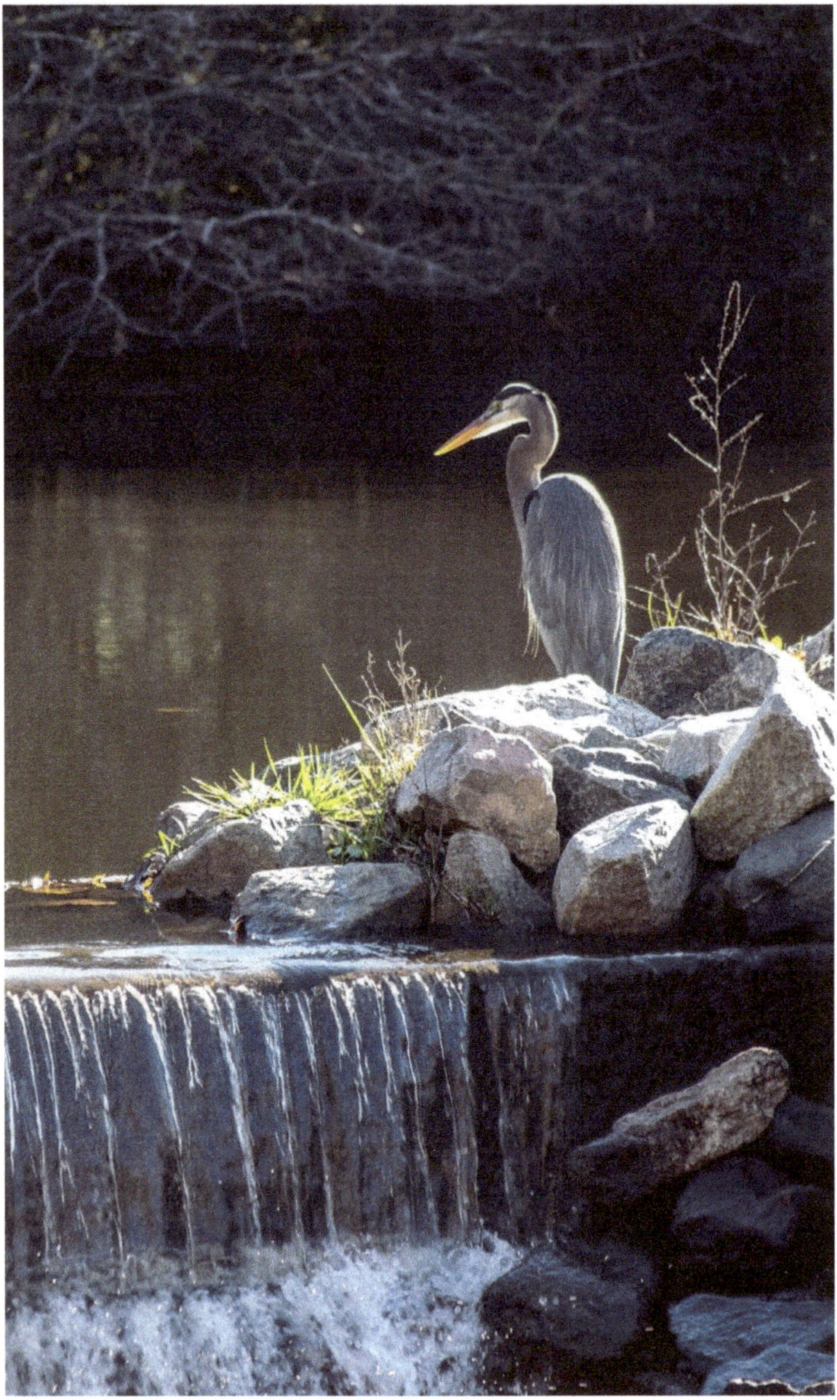

We are strong, confident, and willing to expand our

awareness. Experience life, fearlessly.

Face the future and simply thrive.

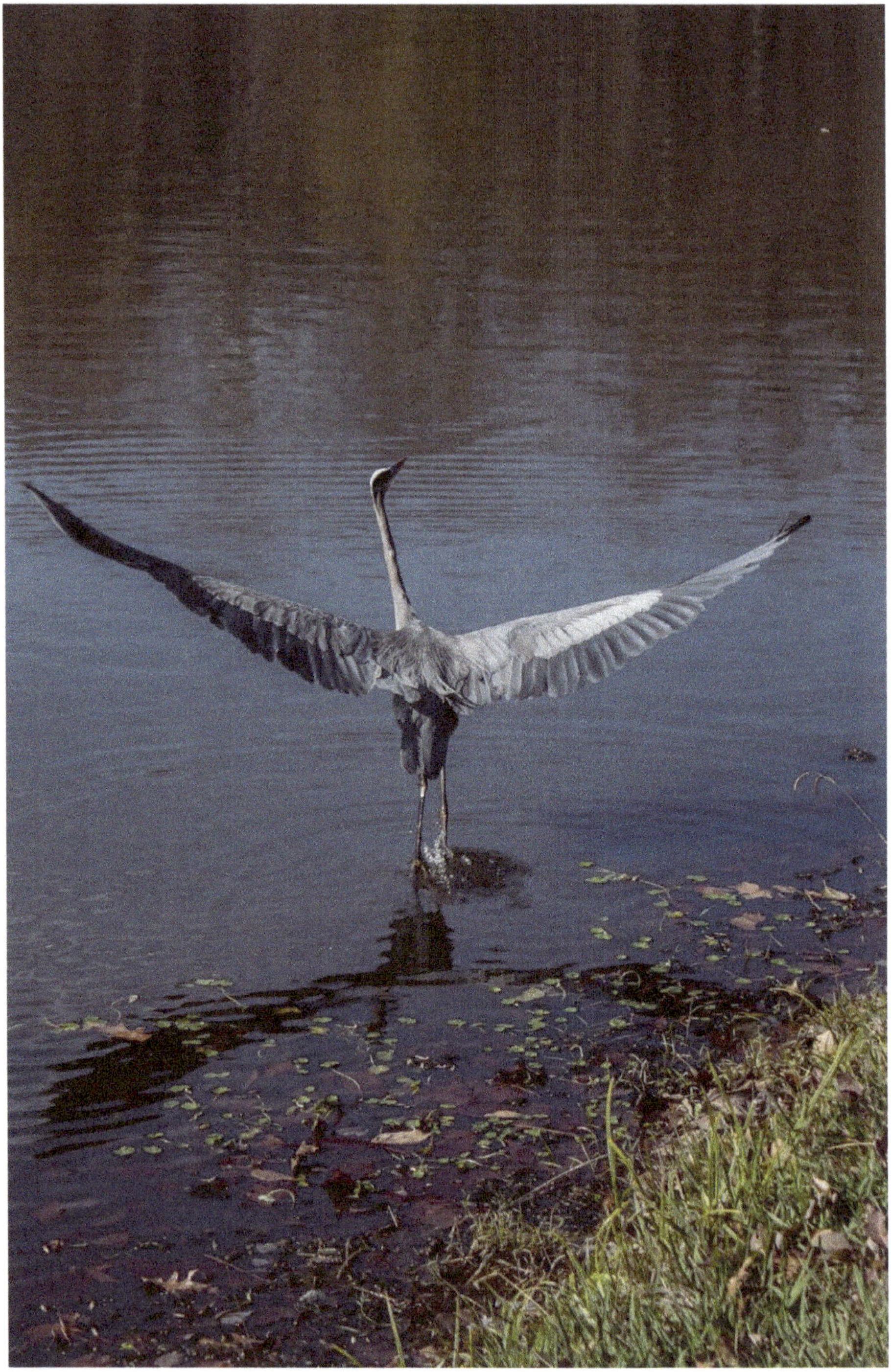

Steady and secure. Life is full of incredible possibilities.

Re-image yourself into positive energy and strength.

Soar, my friend.

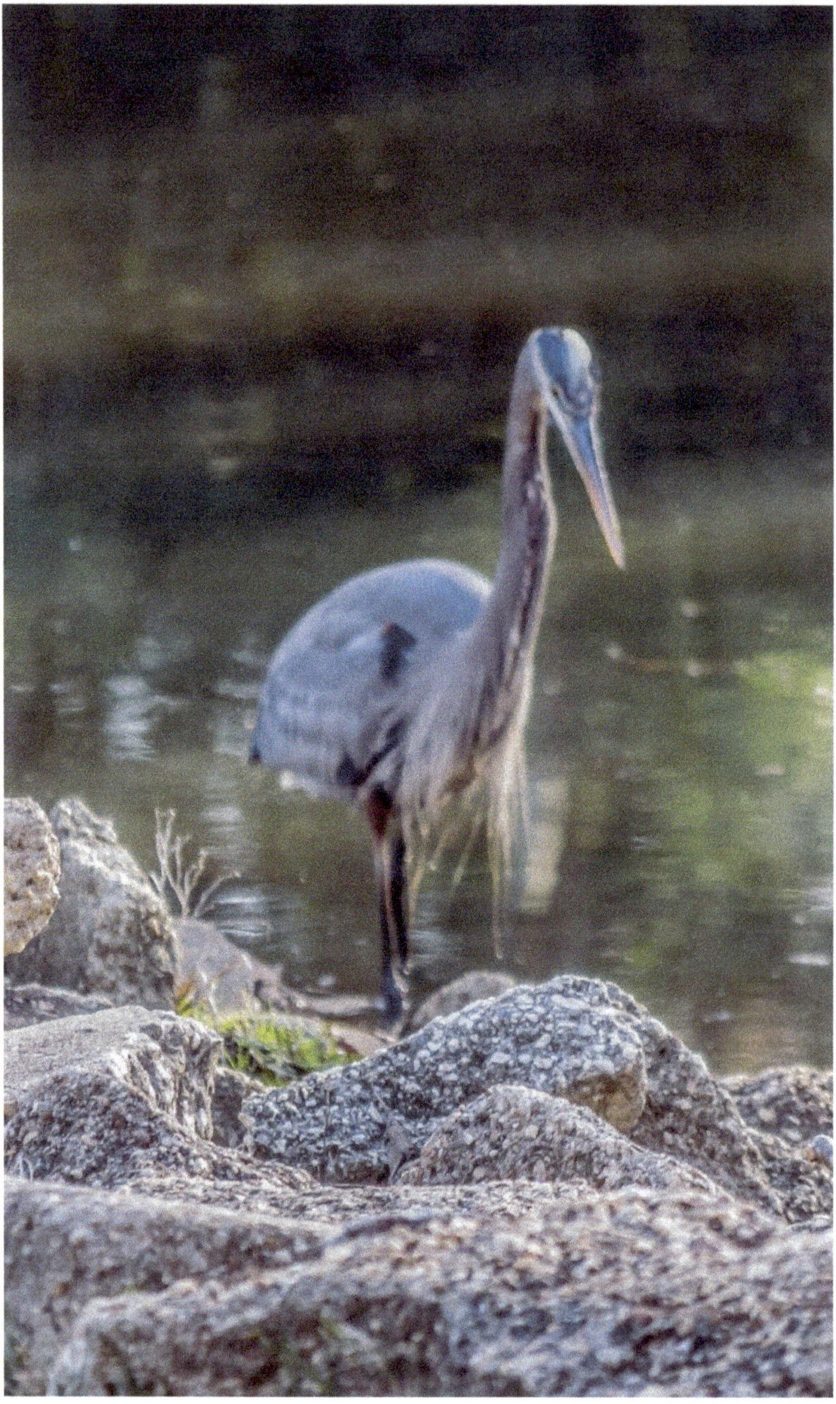

You are great within your being. Radiate confidence and valor as you contemplate your achievements.

Love fully and prosper.

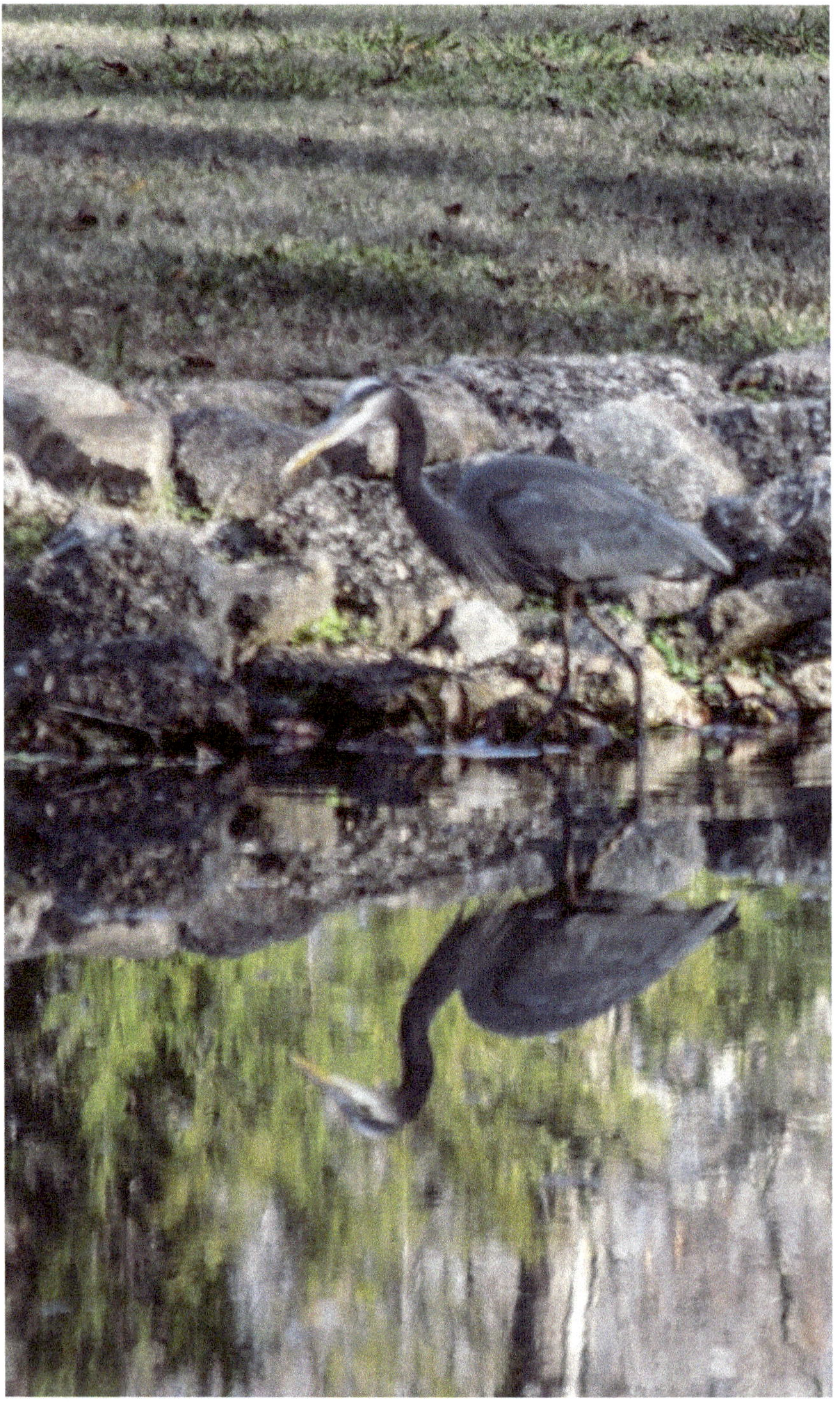

Direct and resilient. Expand your inner strength with grace and beauty. You will be recognized by those who value your existence and understand your worth.

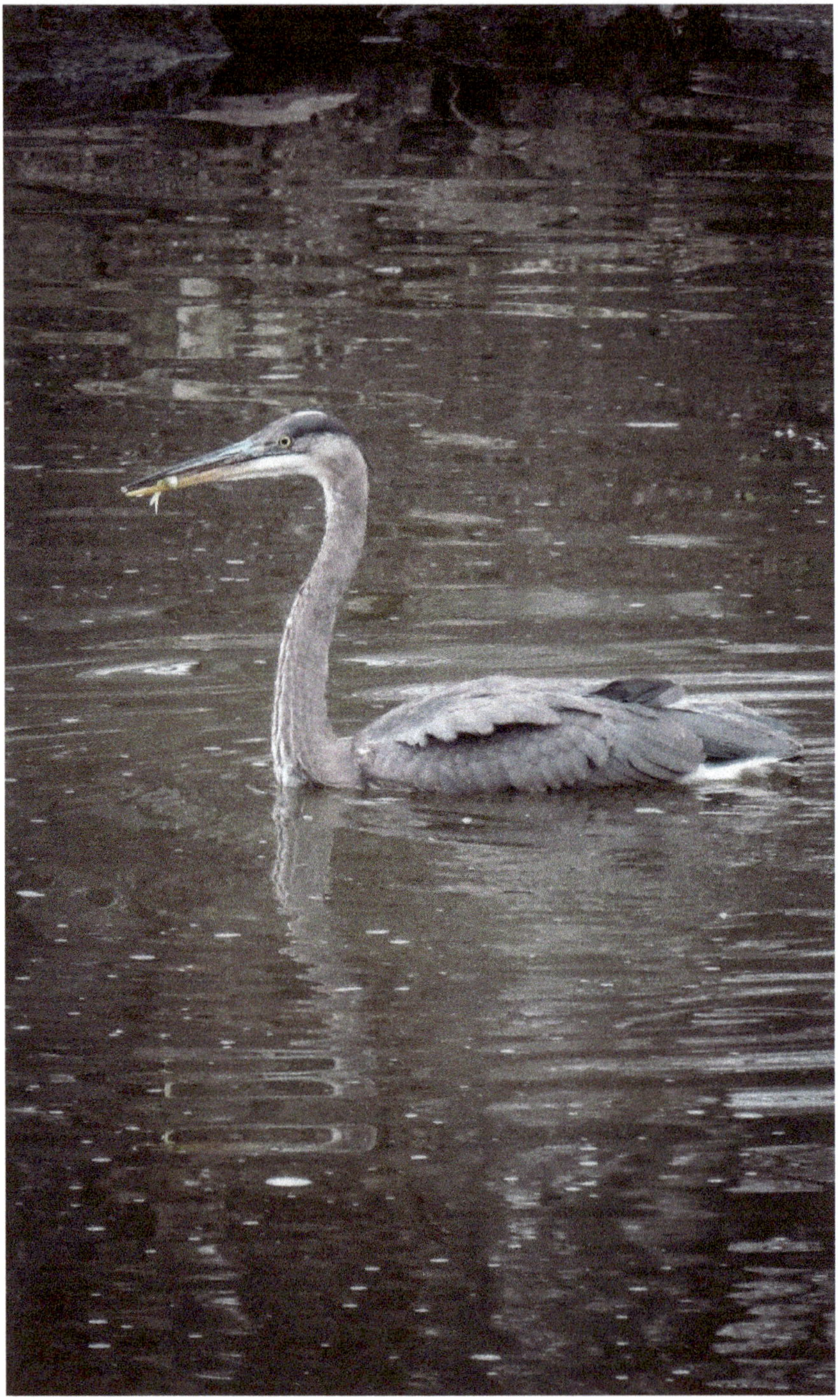

Sometimes we are different and surprise others by our actions. Gliding like a swan may change our presence to a level seldom seen.

Celebrate yourself.

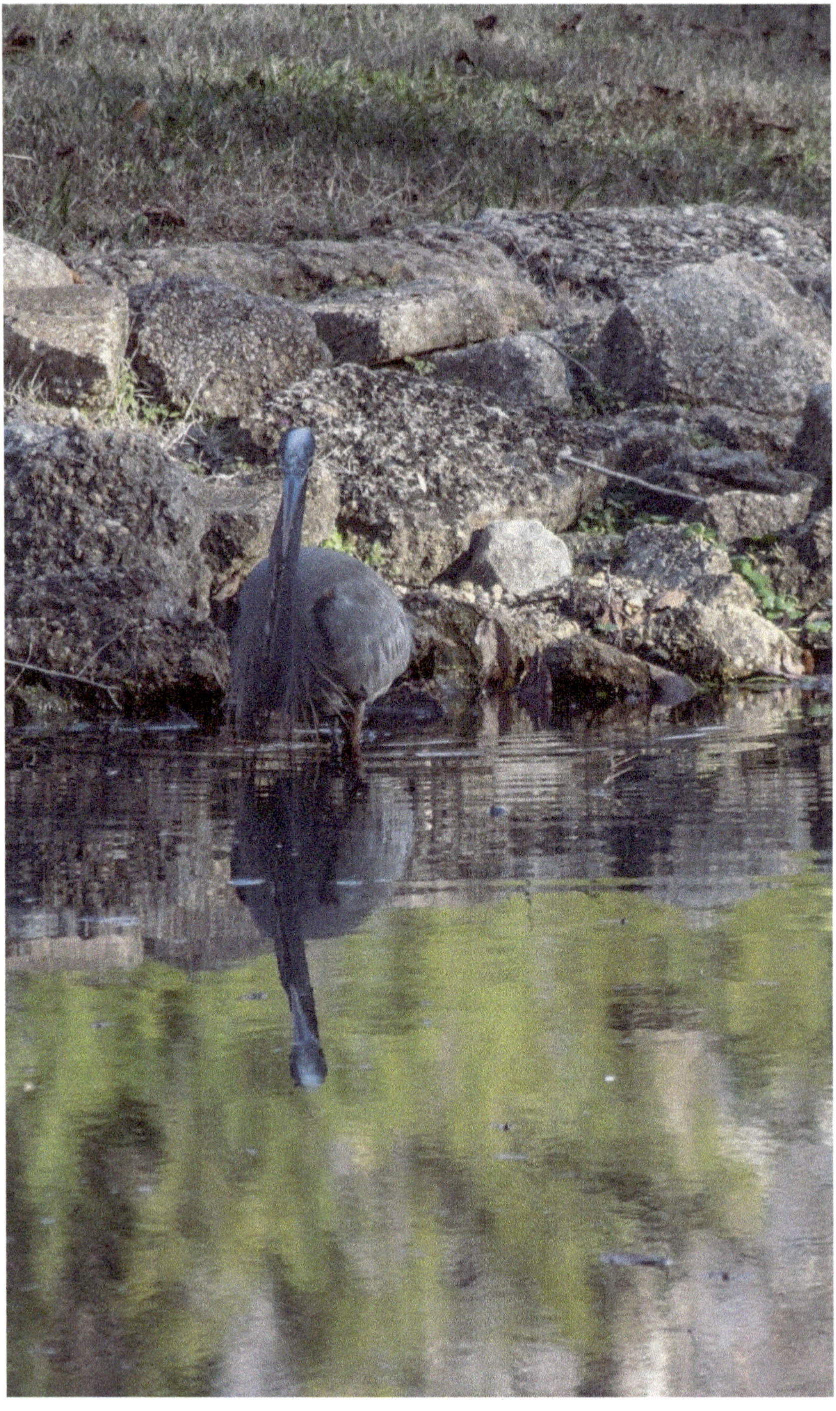

One with nature. Reflect poise, knowledge, and peace within. The beauty of life surrounds your being forever in the shimmering light.

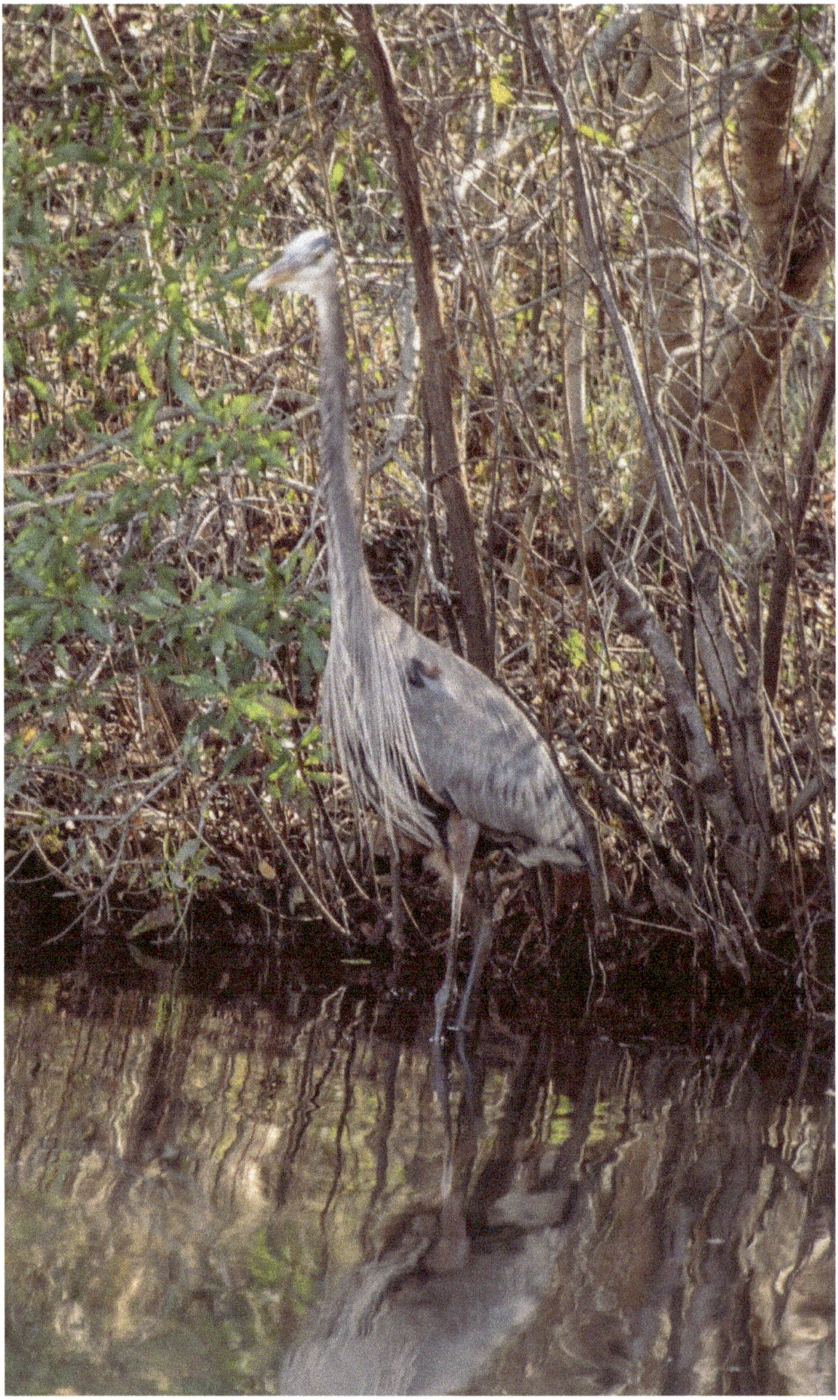

Stand out from the rest. You are unique with the most

valued treasure to share with others

. . . yourself.

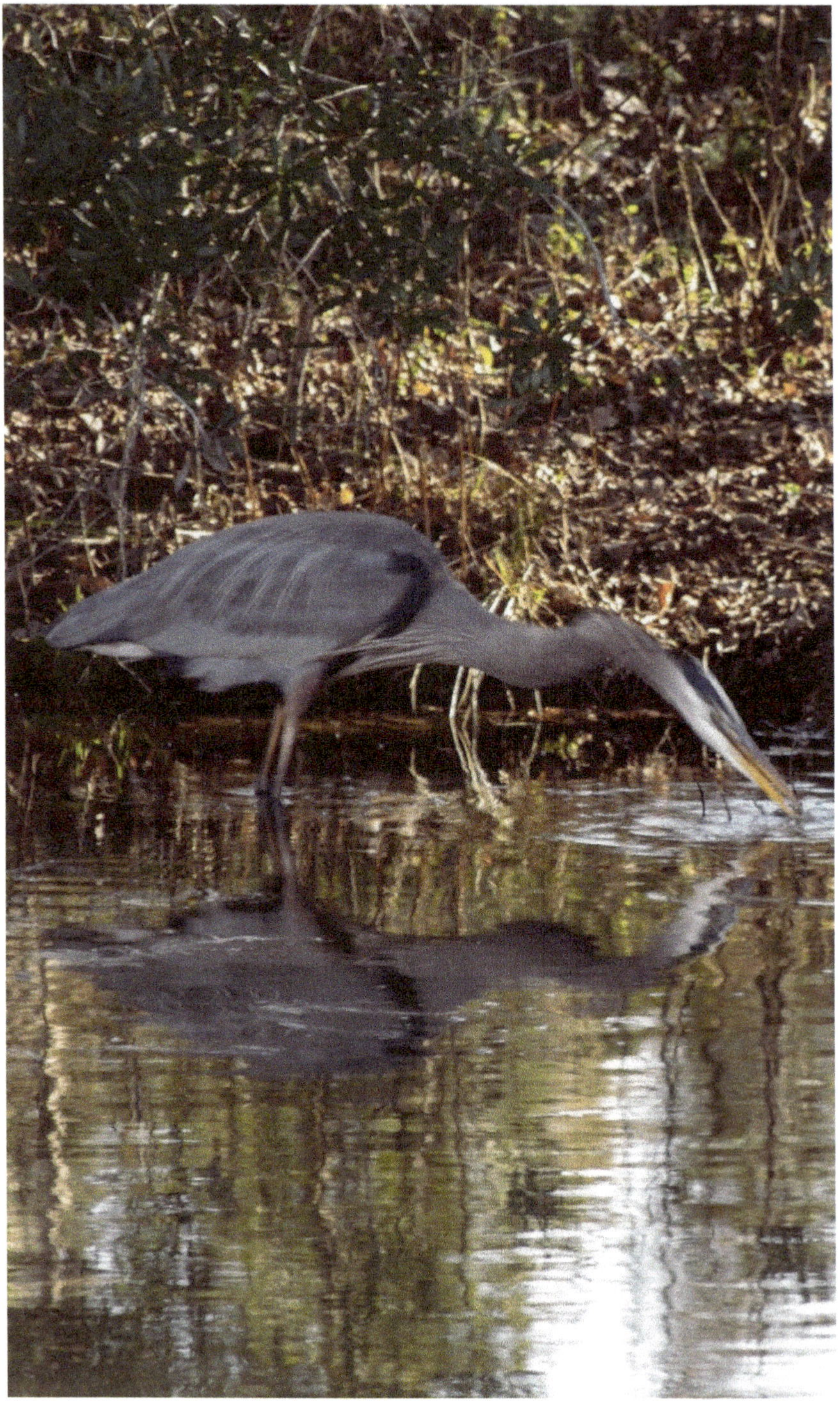

Withstand the elements and continue on your journey.

For life is short and your greatest asset is yet to be . . .

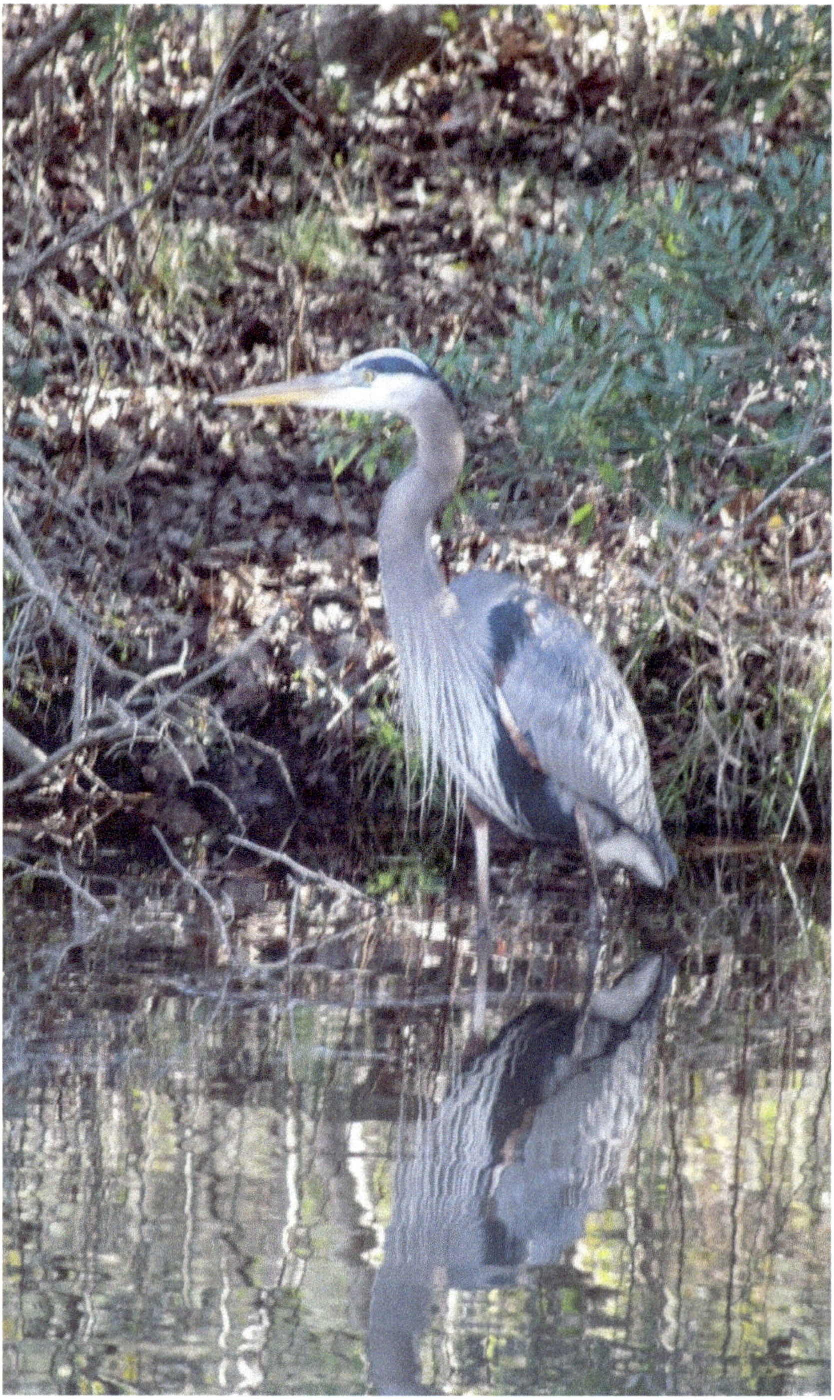

Shades of blue radiate from within. Life is endless with thoughts of you daily. Stay true to your nature and better your existence with the essence of simple beauty.

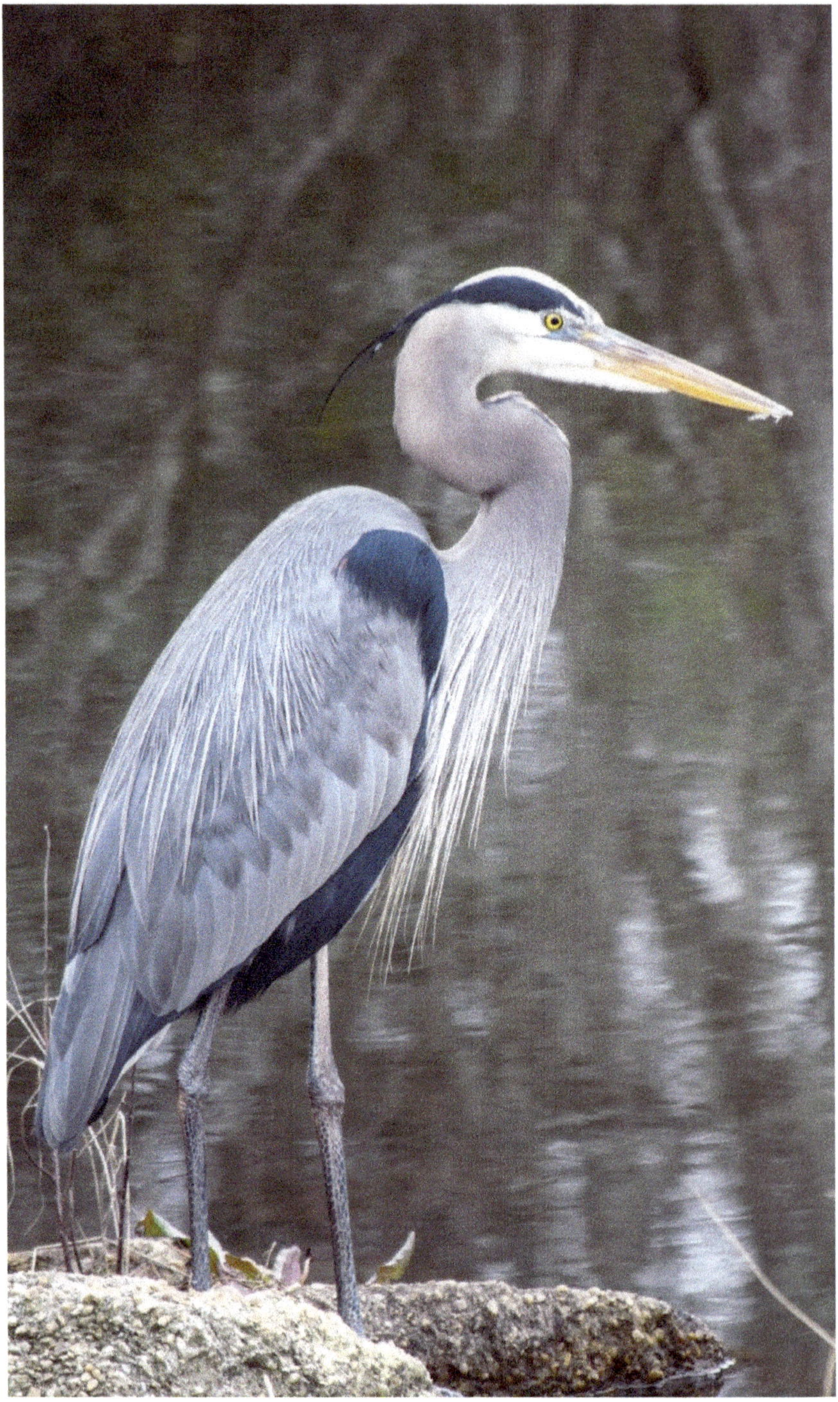

The day is young and so are we. Life surrounds us and makes us complete. We are perfect within.

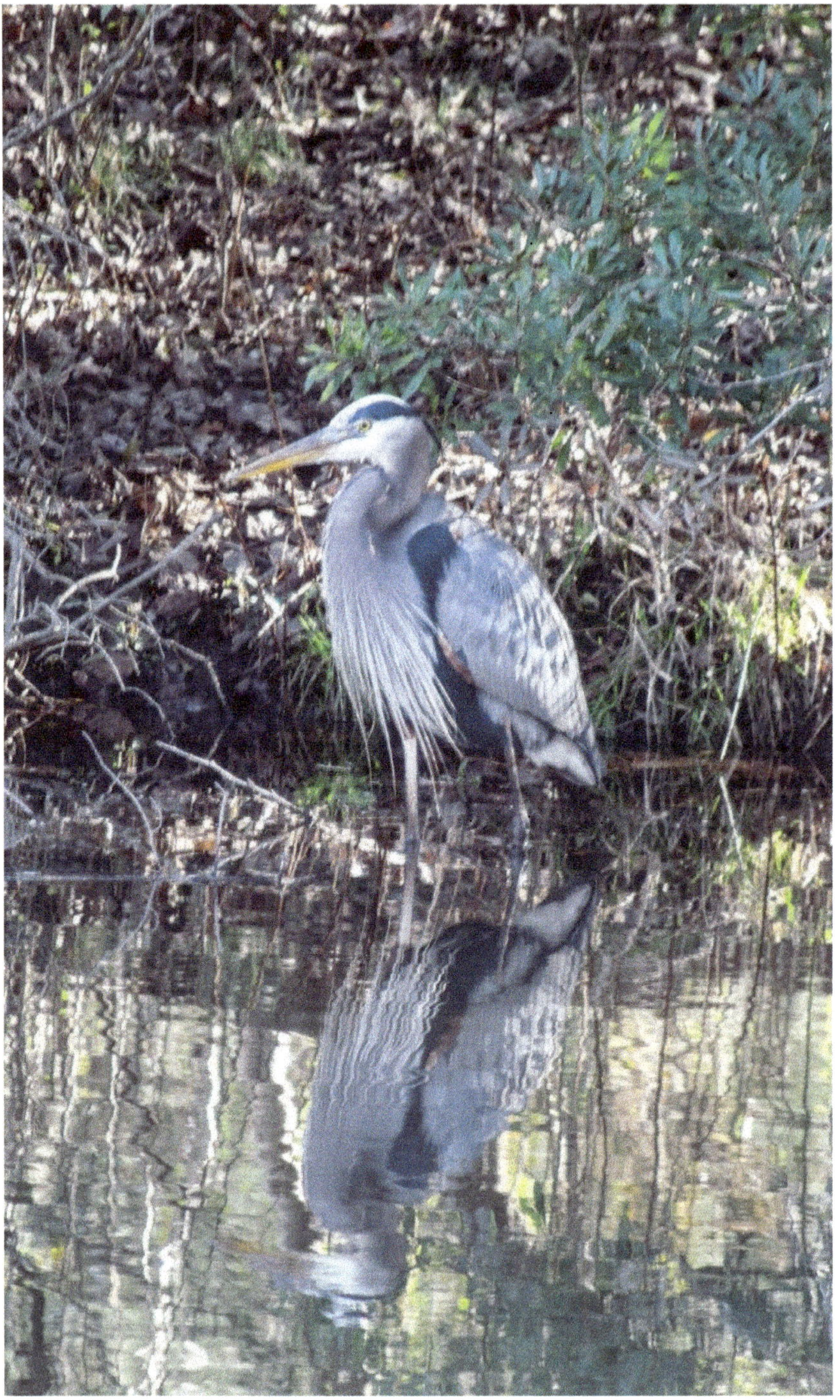

Do your best to reap new experiences. Grow with strength, courage, and resilience. You will be amazed by your speed.

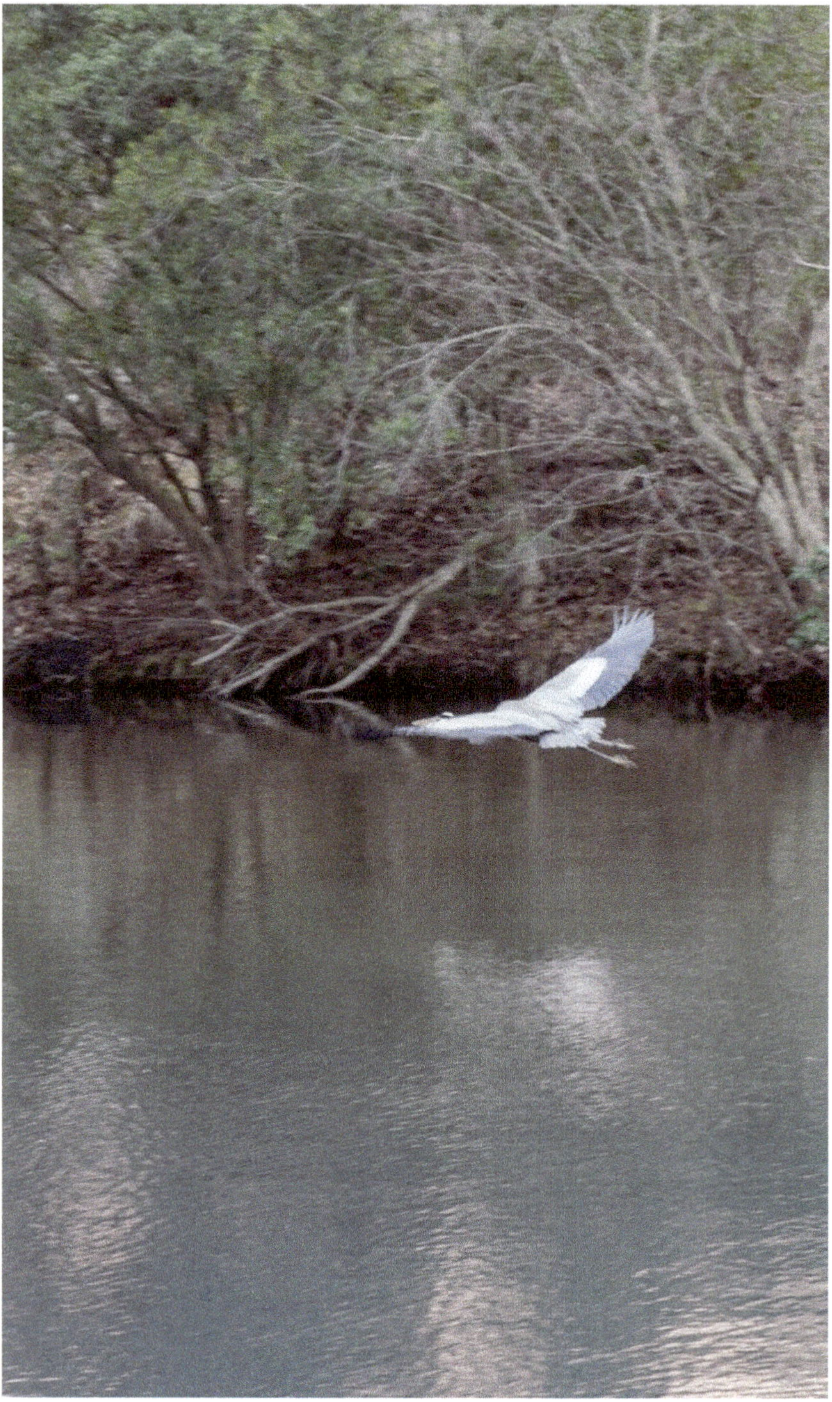

Be free. No obstacle is too great. The warmth of the sun is never forgotten. Tomorrow will follow with unknown joy.

Revere life.

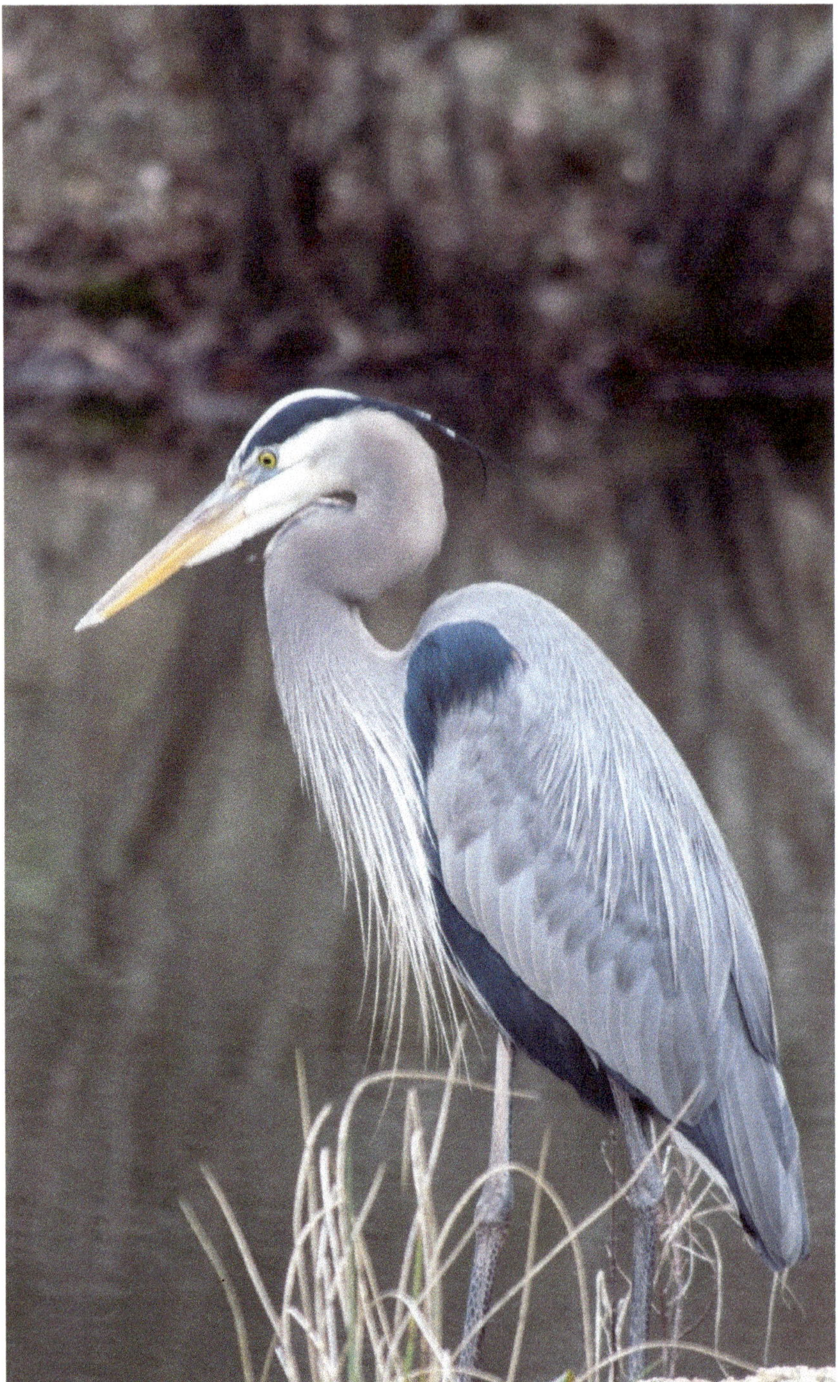

Beauty is blending naturally in nature. We see beauty, we sense beauty, and we are beautifully complete.

Enjoy the moment.

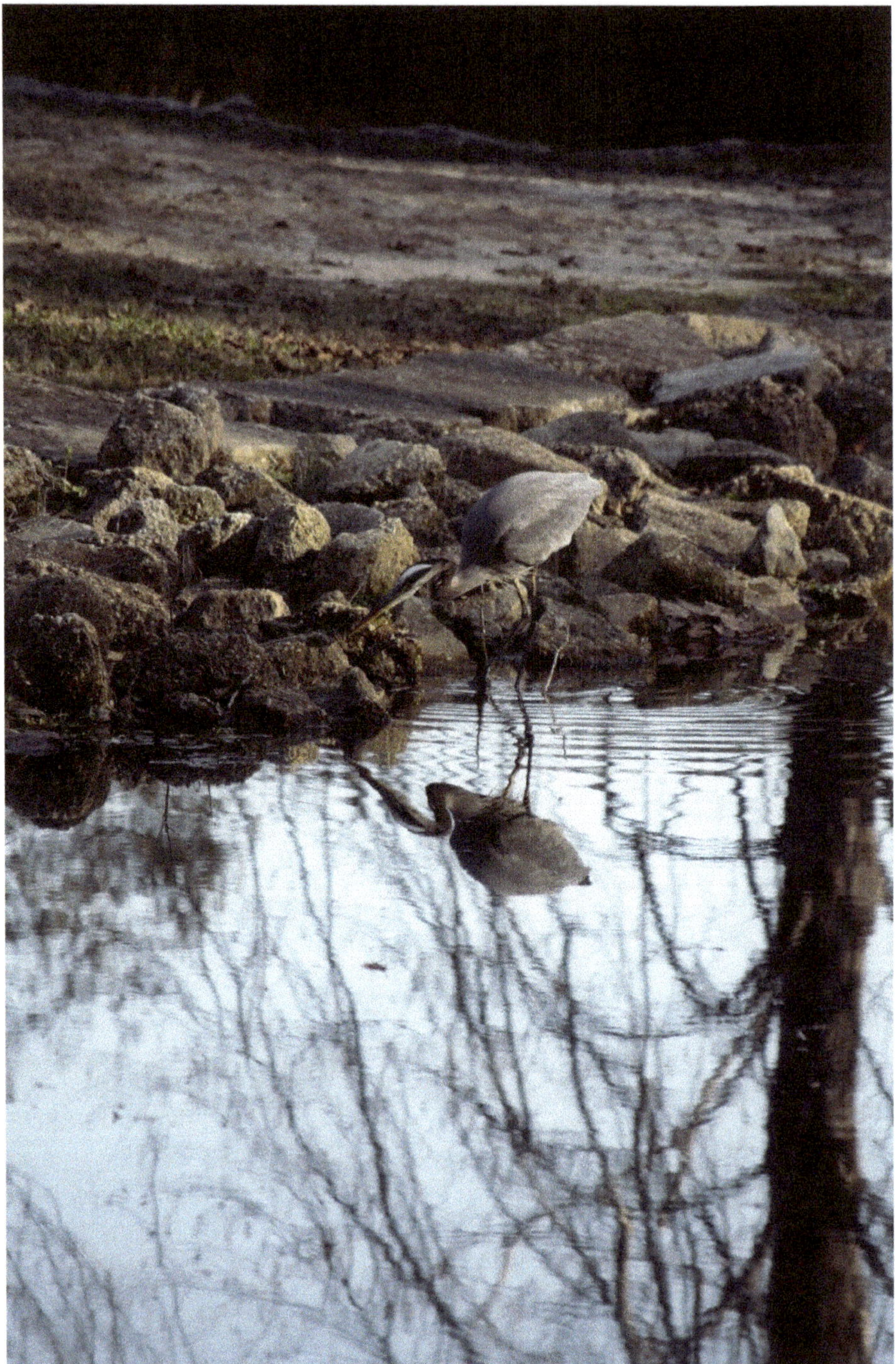

Look closely from a fresh perspective. Life unfolds on the other side. Wondrous and full. Follow the ripples of unexplored adventures yet to be.

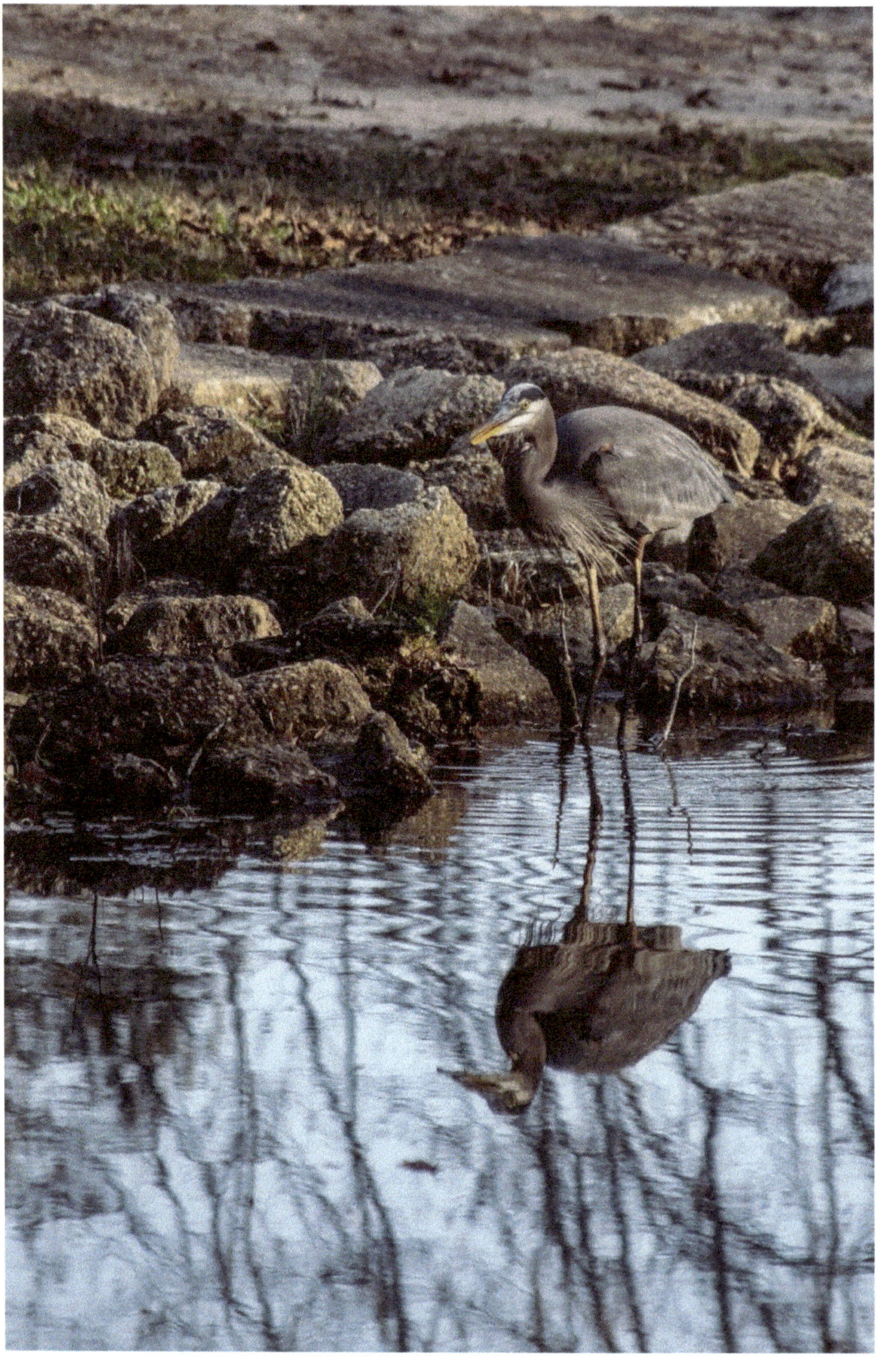

The taller we stand, the wider our vision of a greater tomorrow. Never lose faith in what can be, dear friend.

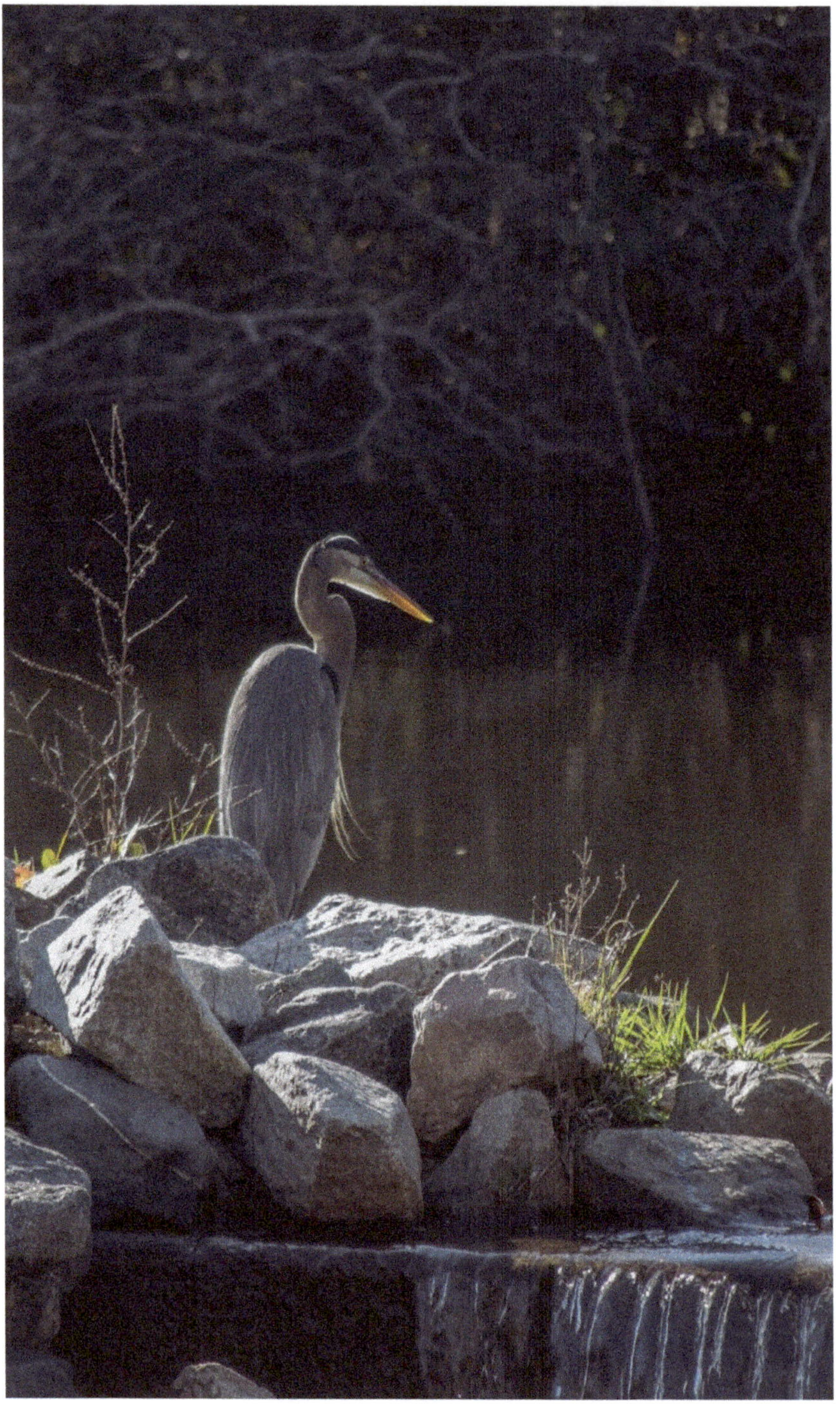

On the edge of stillness, feel empowered with self-worth and wonder. Look past your image and see mine.

Glorious.

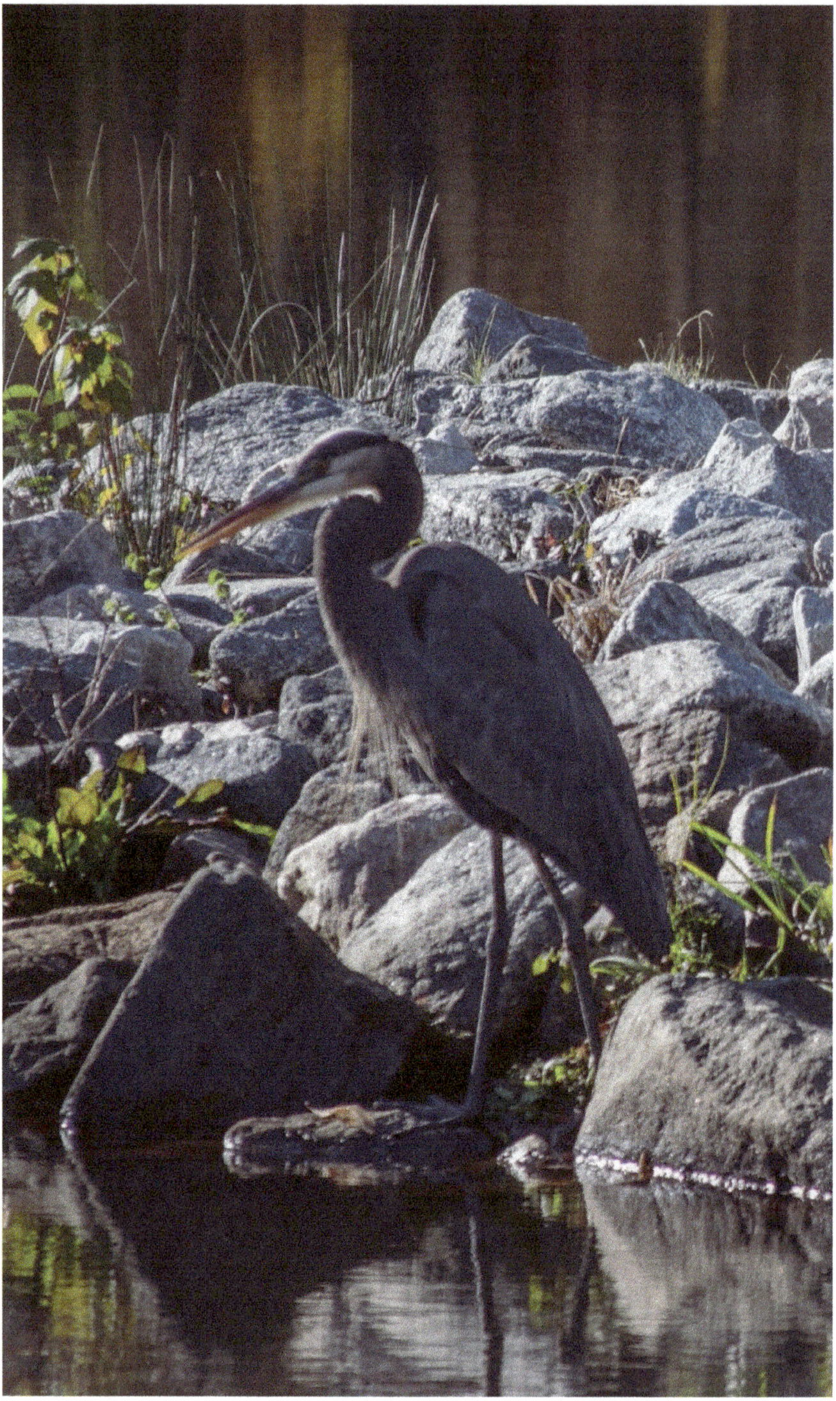

The shadows are falling all around us, and yet, we thrive.

Our essence shines in the incoming darkness of night.

To be alive is enough.

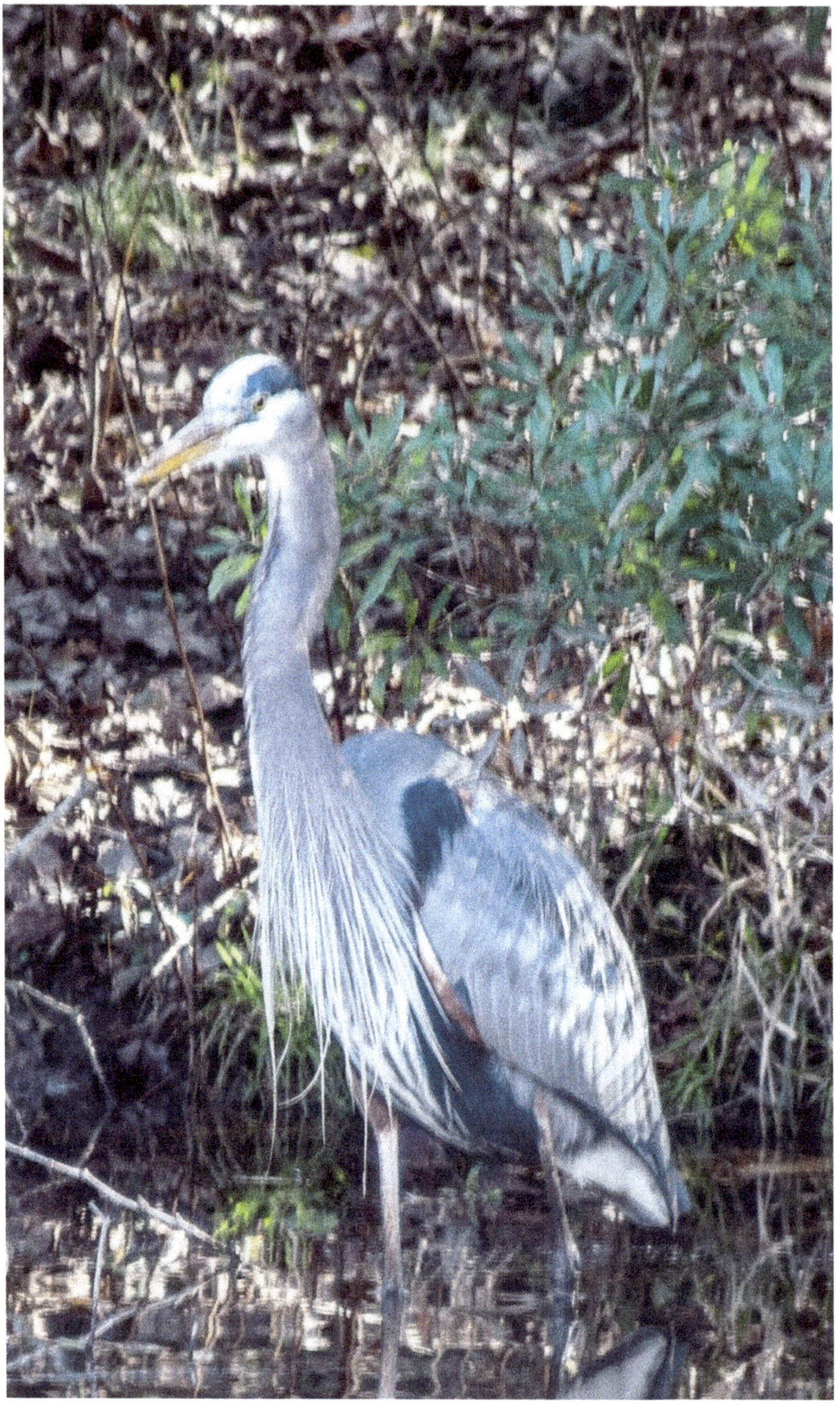

Balance your weaknesses with amazing strengths.

Personal growth is astonishing.

You are admired from afar, constantly.

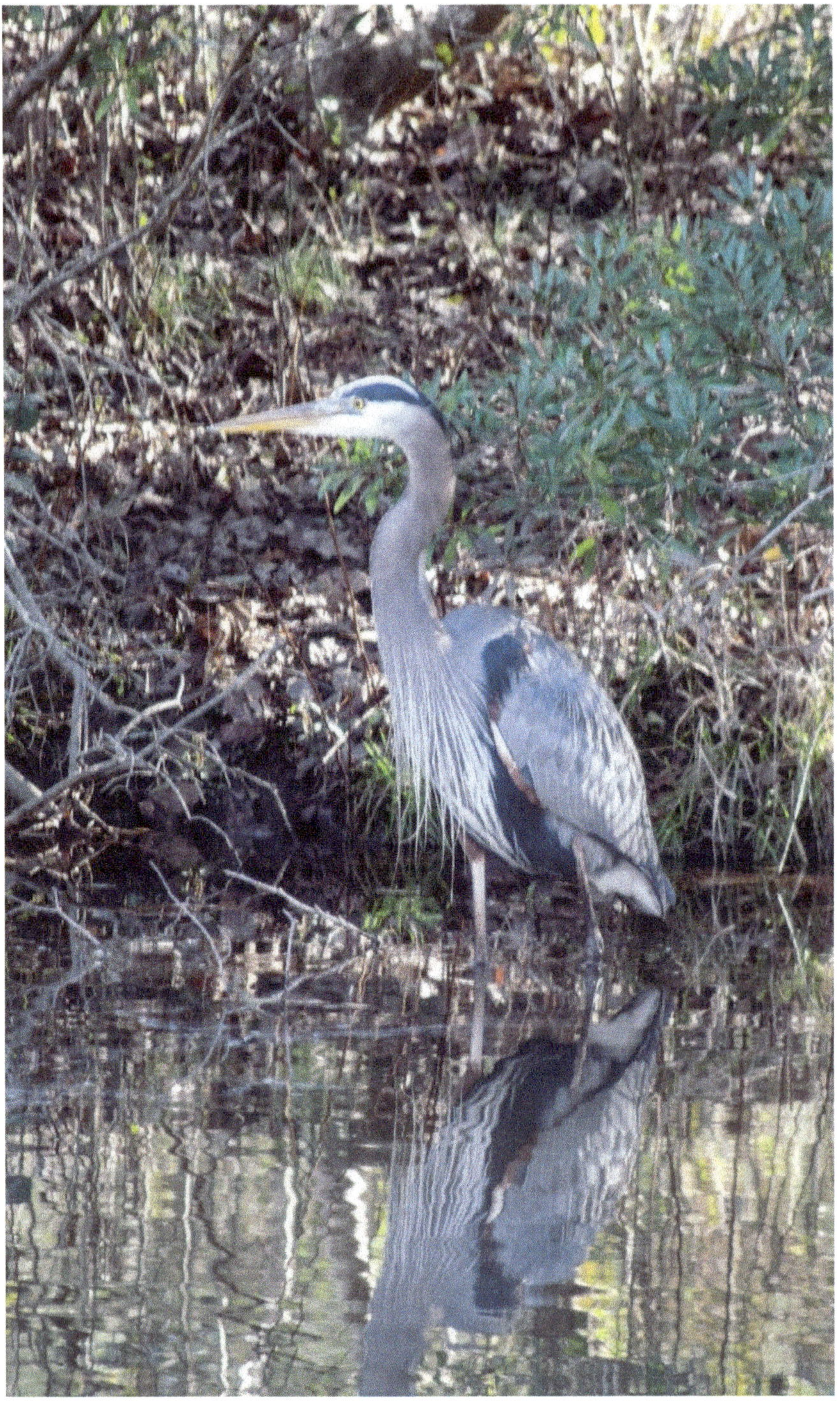

Stand firm and proud. In the background, learn many lessons. In the foreground, become an inspiring leader. Change is inevitable and certain.

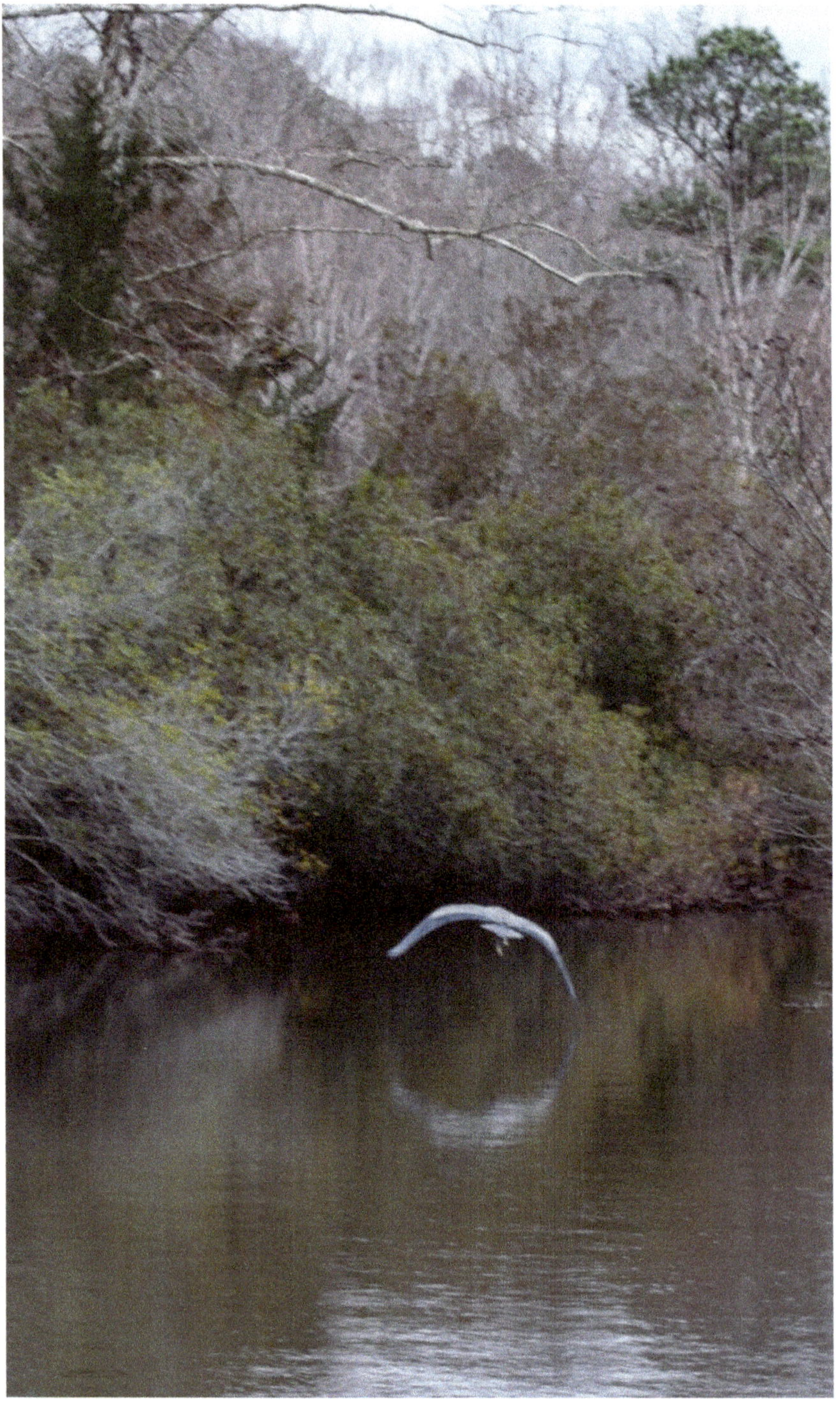

We will glide gently to our destination. Greatness is in the making of yet another day. Contentment will follow.

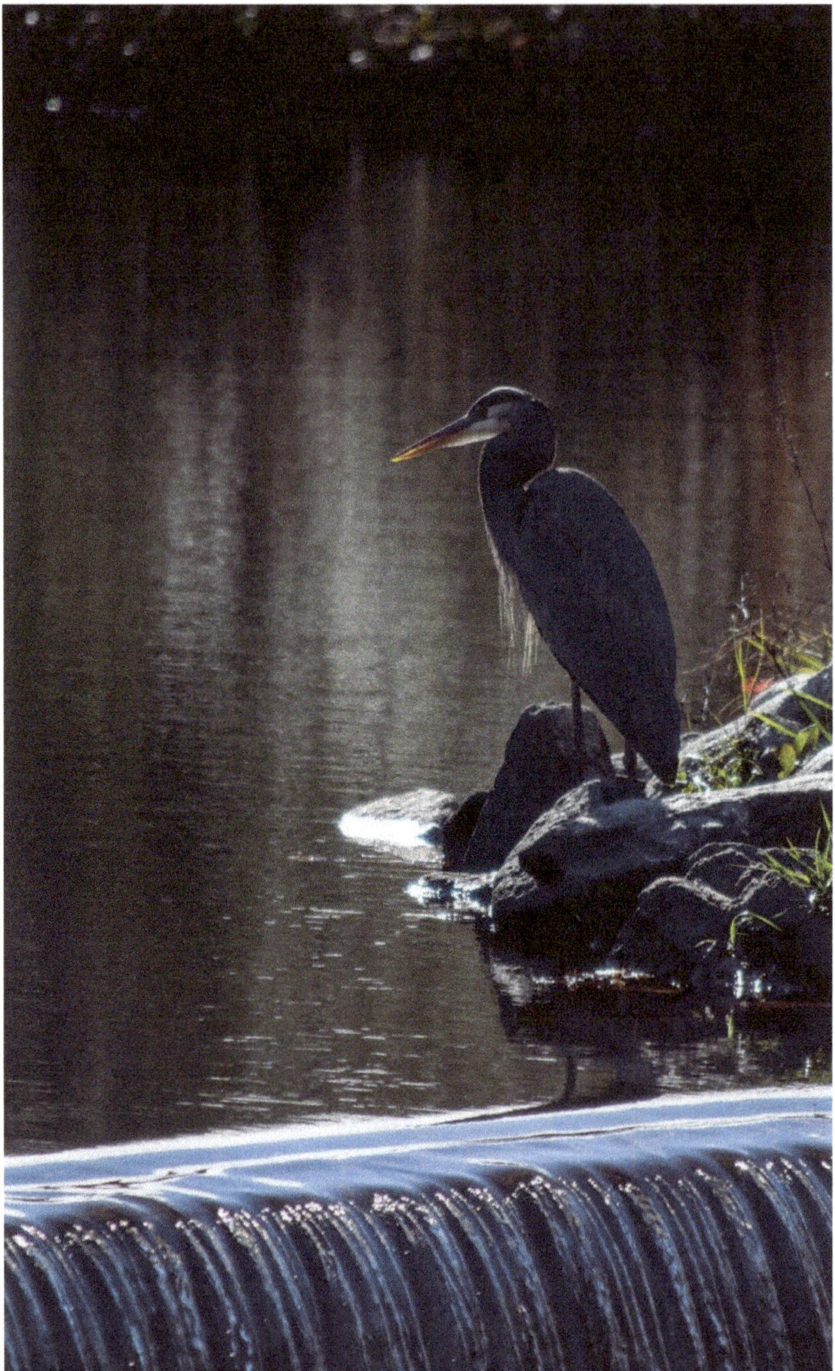

Daylight is dwindling. The light reflects a new beginning tomorrow. Stand ready for the brightness of life and what will become you.

Shimmer.

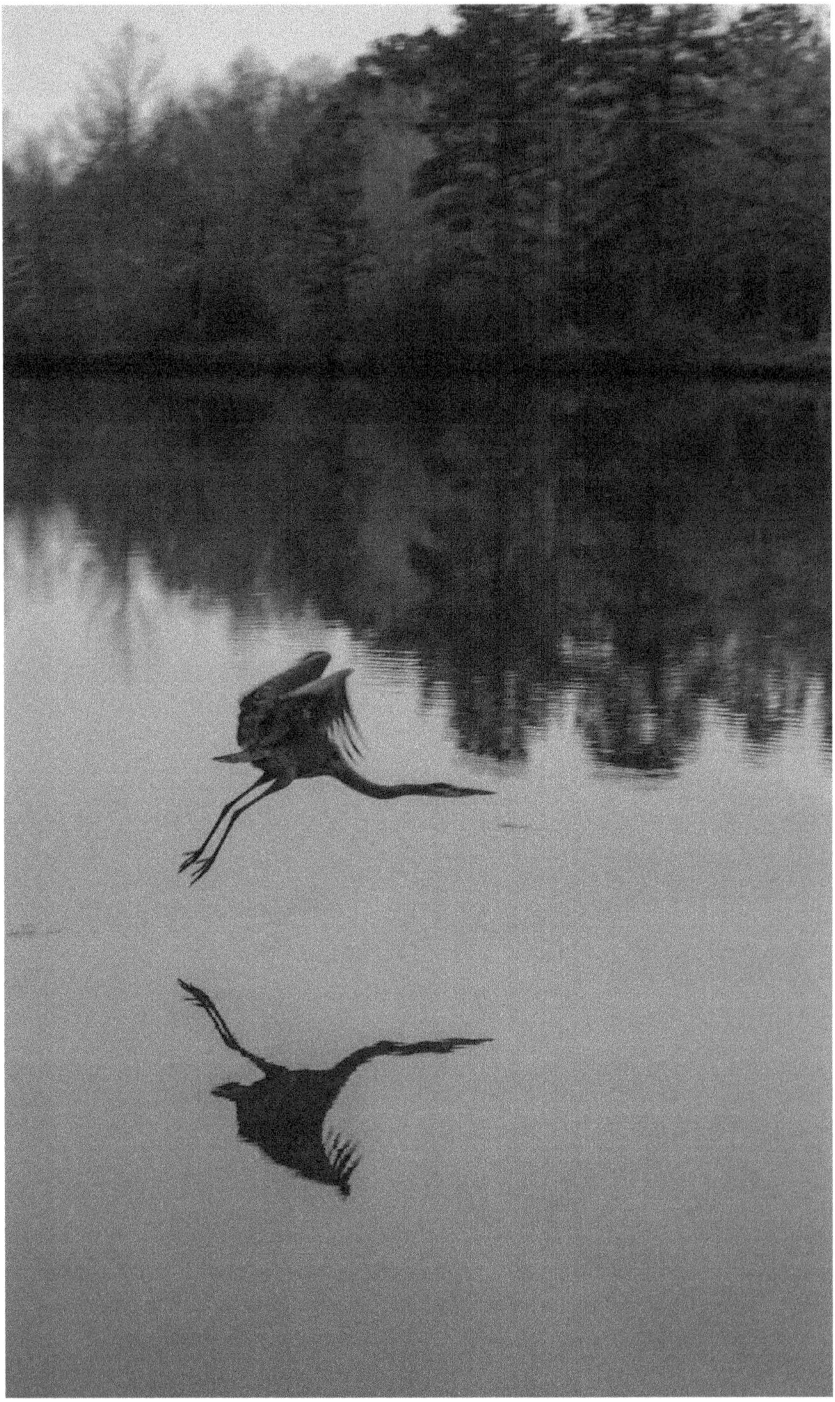

Characterize us by determination, agility, and spirit.

Appreciate the unique stance we bring to the world.

Take us home . . .

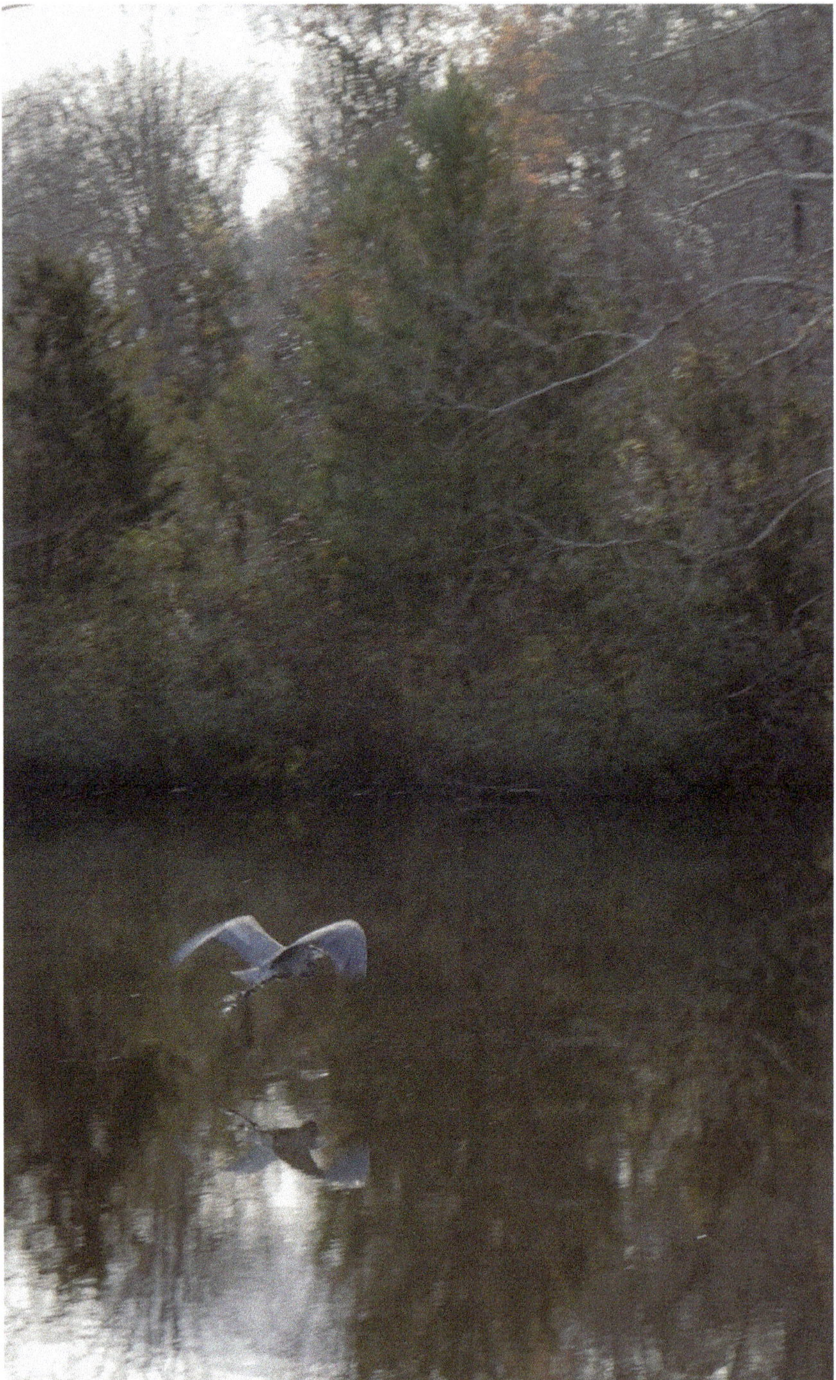

Free and uplifting. This instant in time is glorious.

Reflective in nature. Enjoy the freedom.

Momentous.

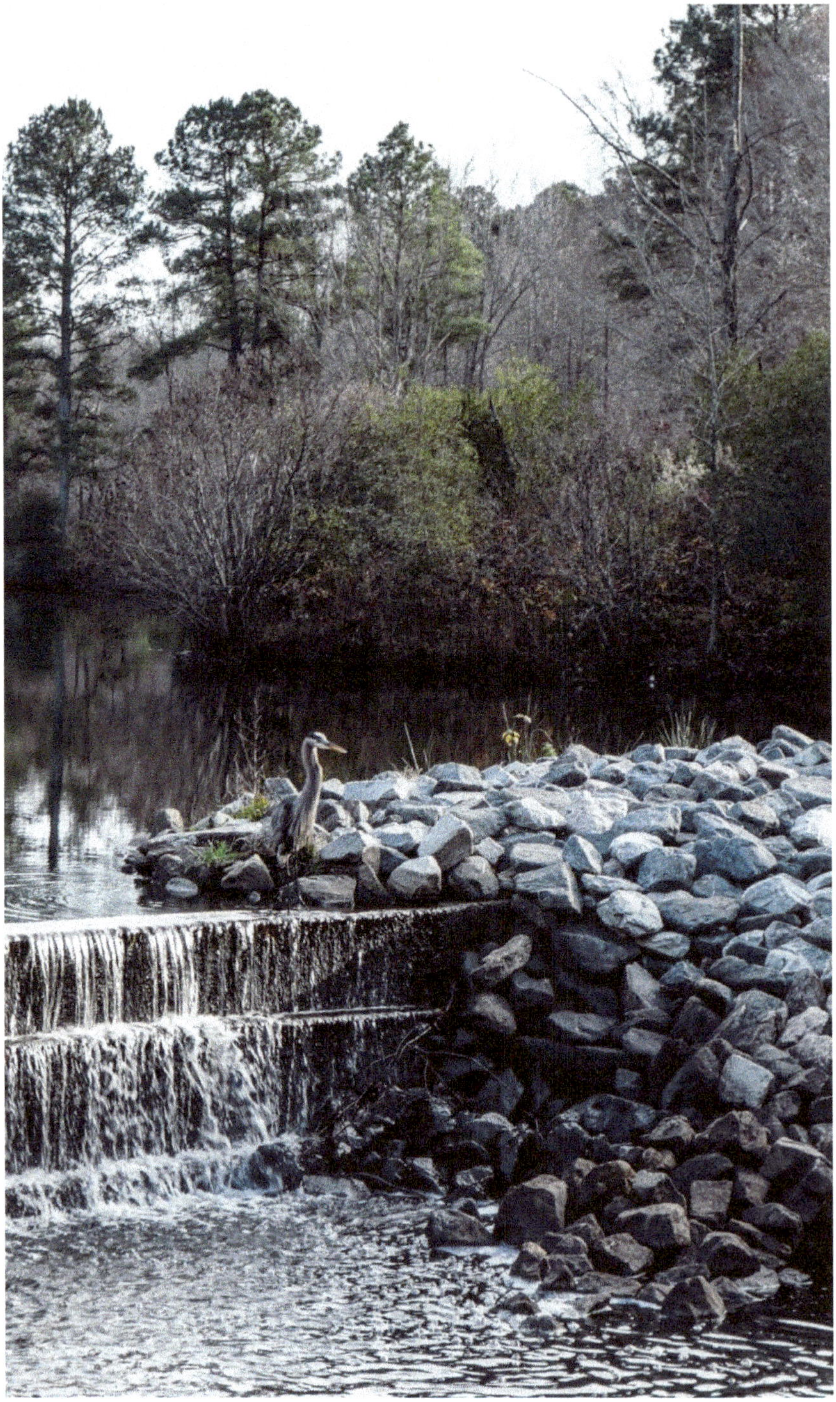

Shine through nature's beauty with grace and elegance.

Life awaits your presence.

You are divine.

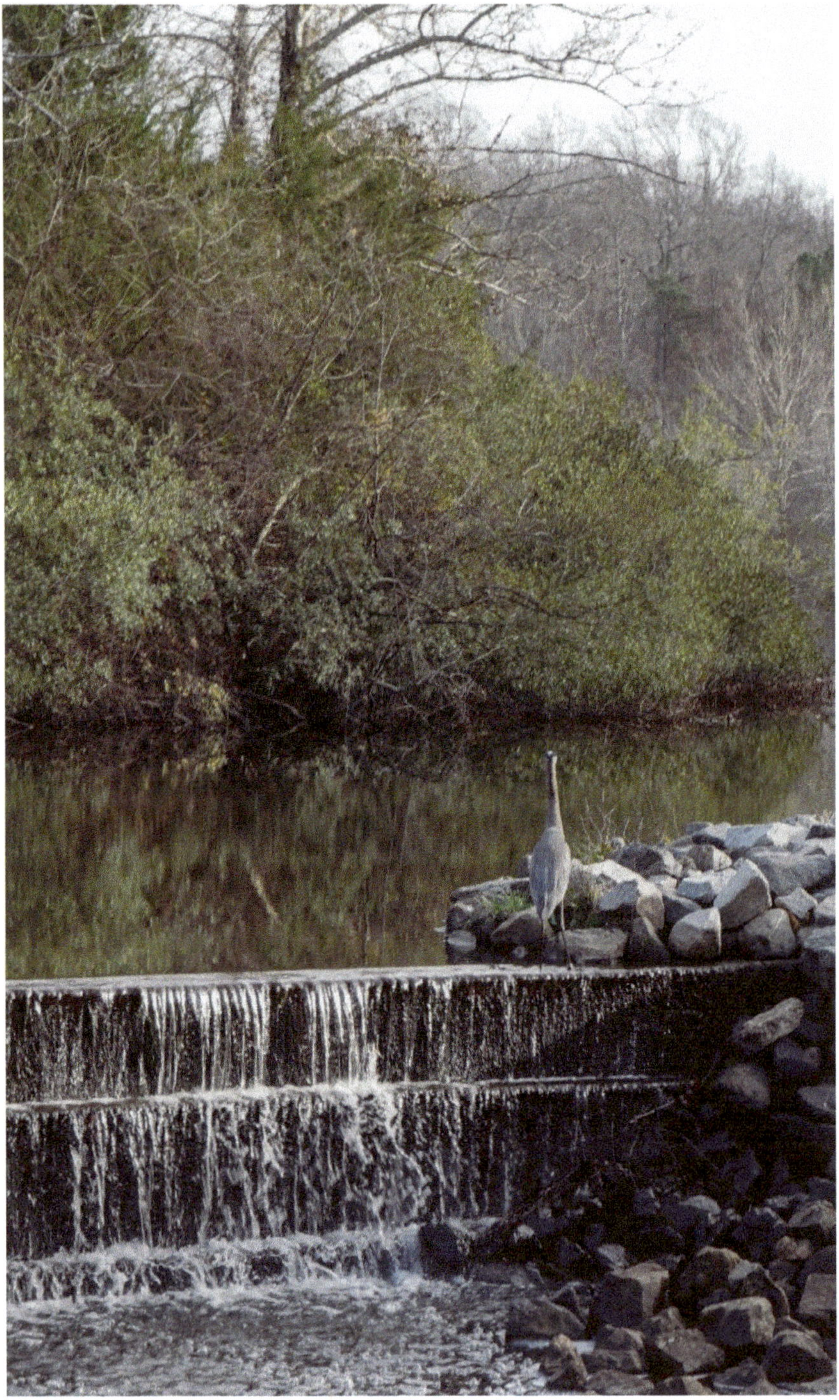

Towering on the rocks. Secure footing is needed for a lifetime of intrigue and adoration. Be one with yourself and radiate peaceful moments within.

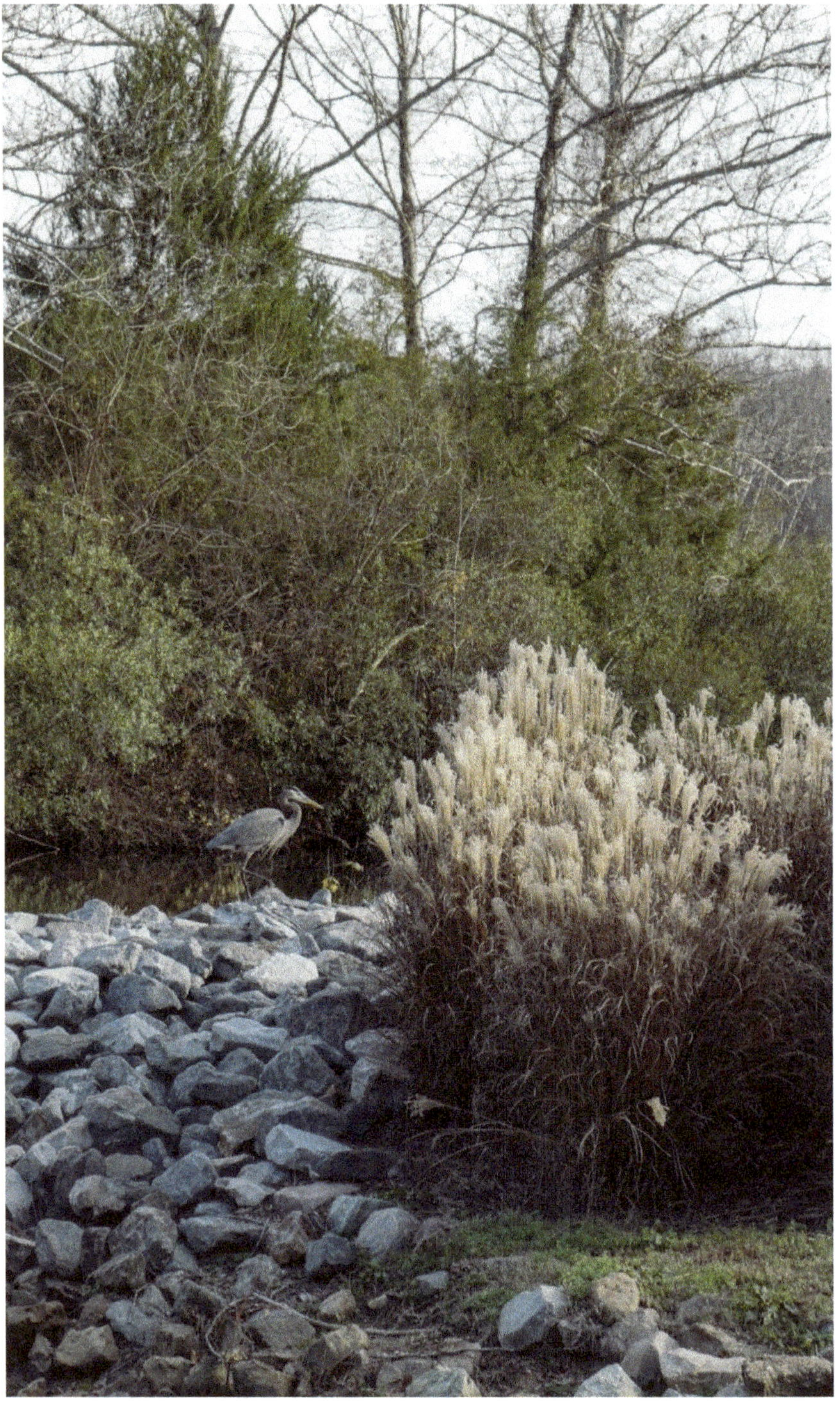

Never hesitate to follow the journey. Know that success shadows your decisions and thoughts with stamina and confidence. Share strength with others.

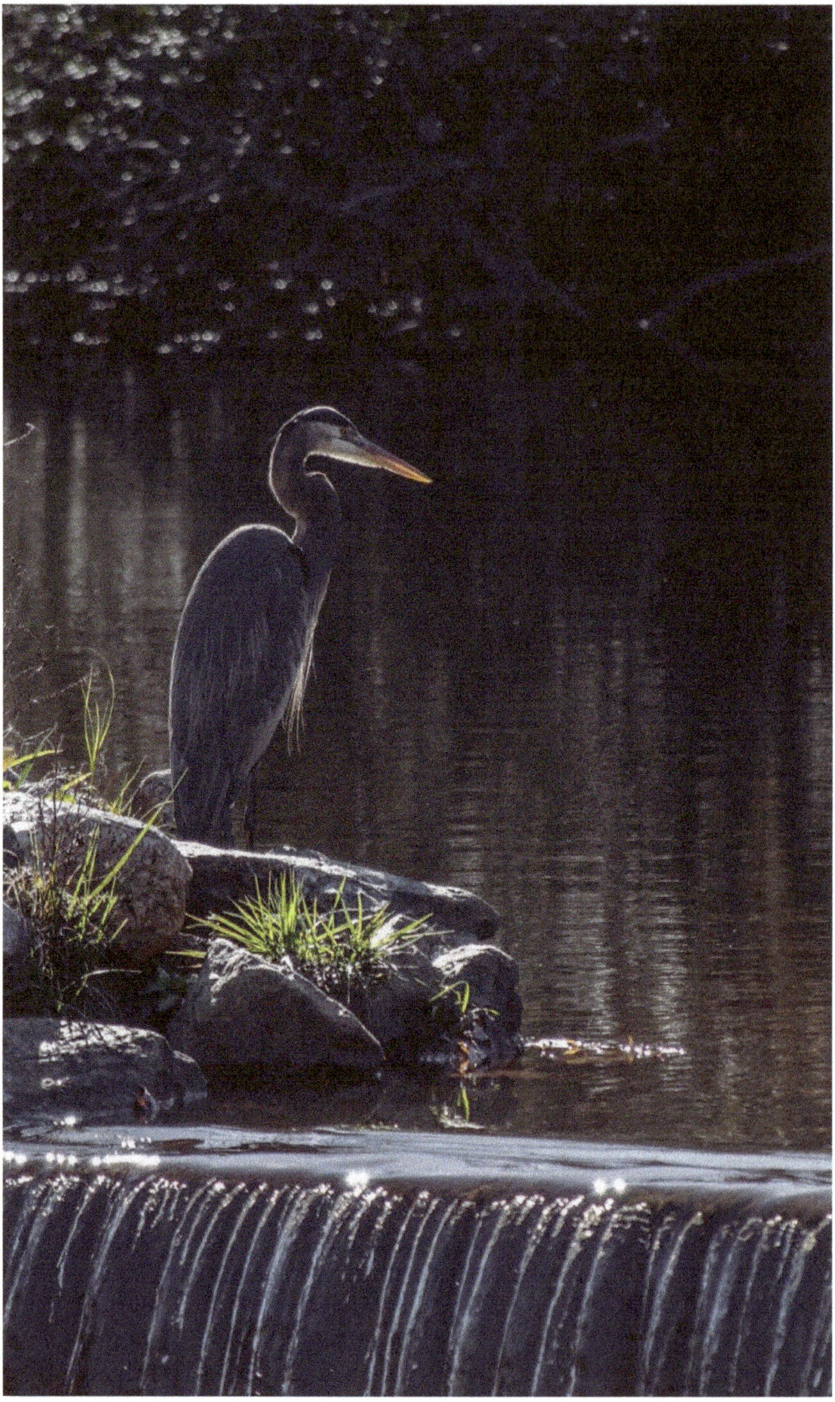

The makeup of the moment is perfect. Being part of a greater whole is calling. Appreciate the treasured time, together.

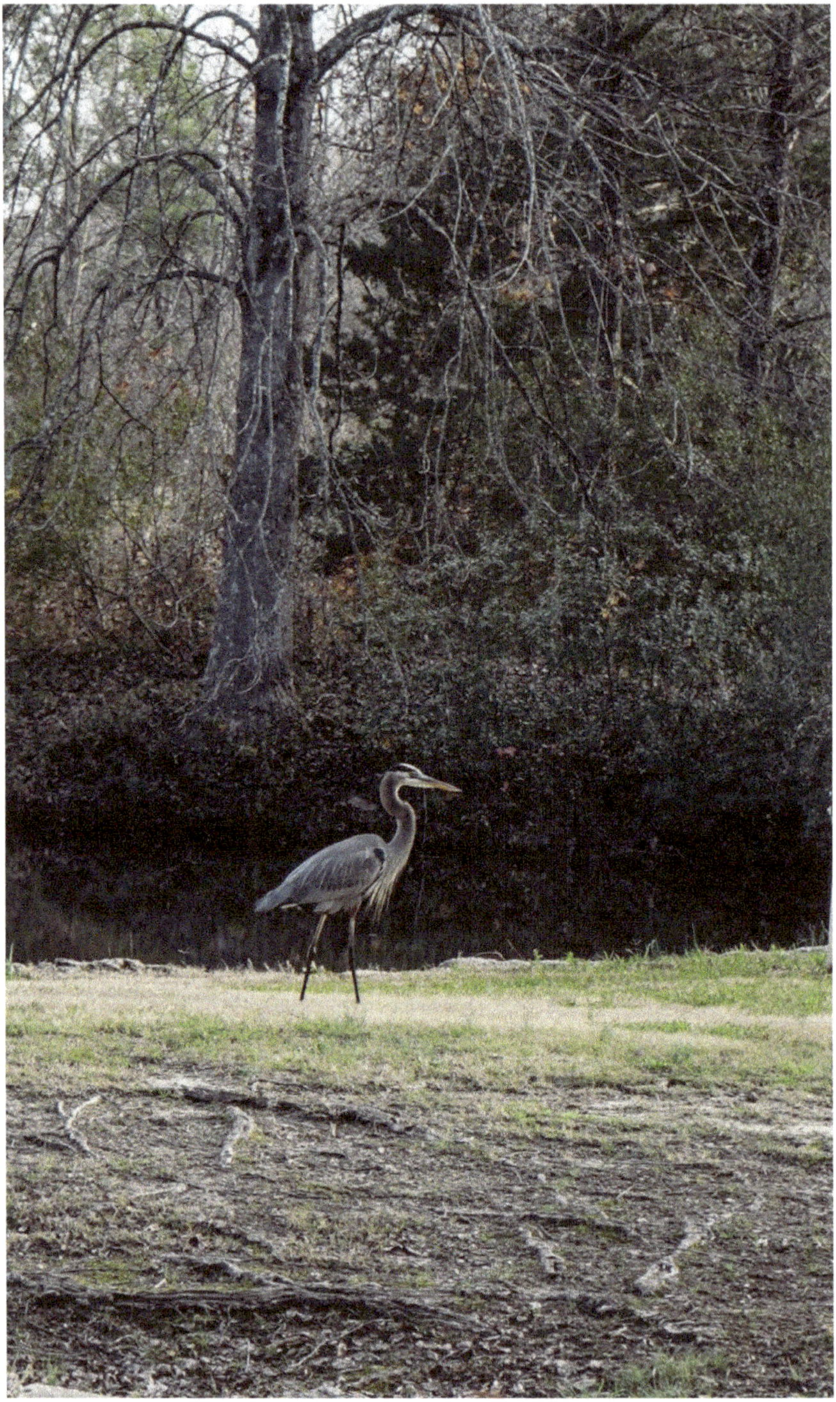

Follow the signs of nature ensuring victory in your future. Make significant strides forward. Build confidence and strength with every step.

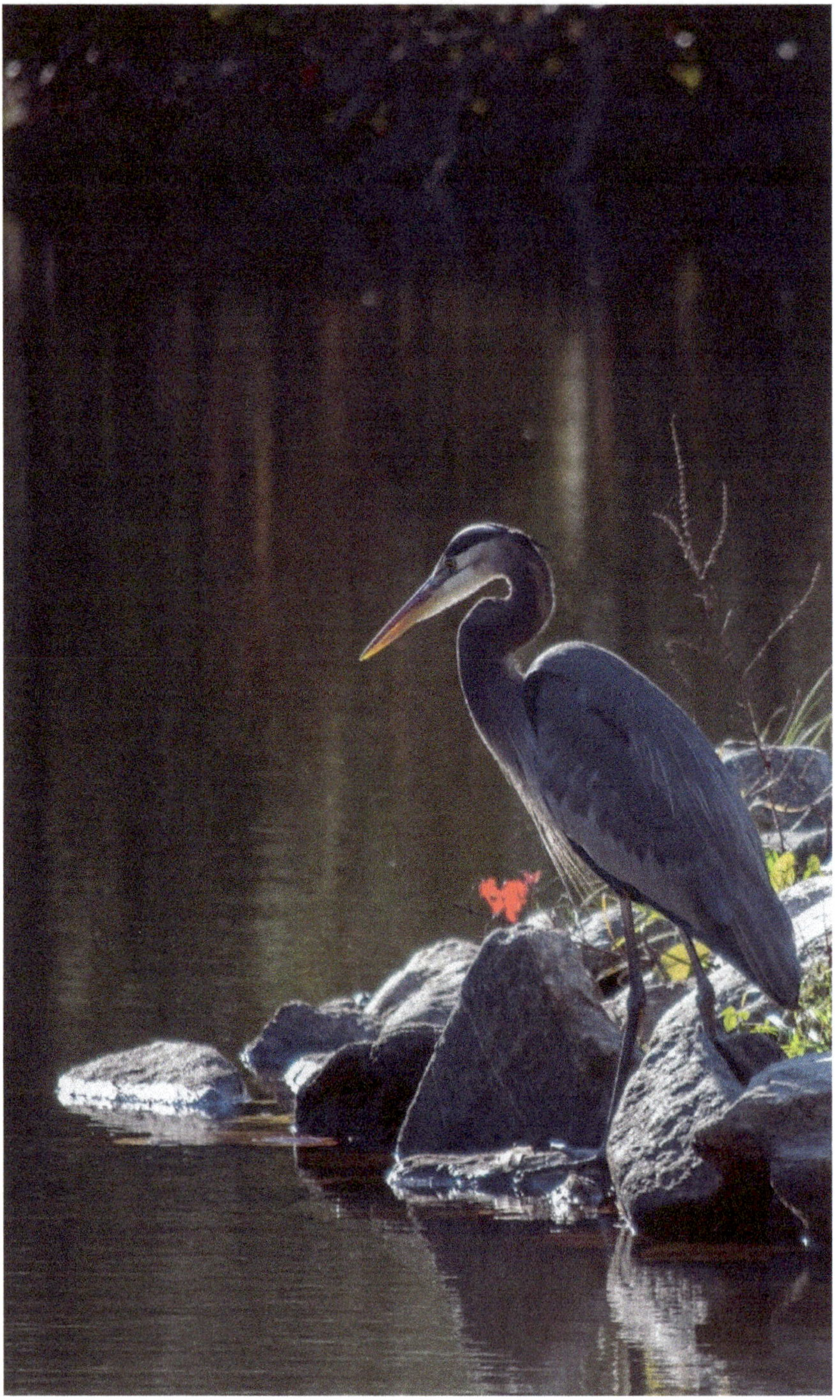

The red leaf adorns our being. We are part of the tapestry of life. The heart is pure and forgiving, unconditionally.

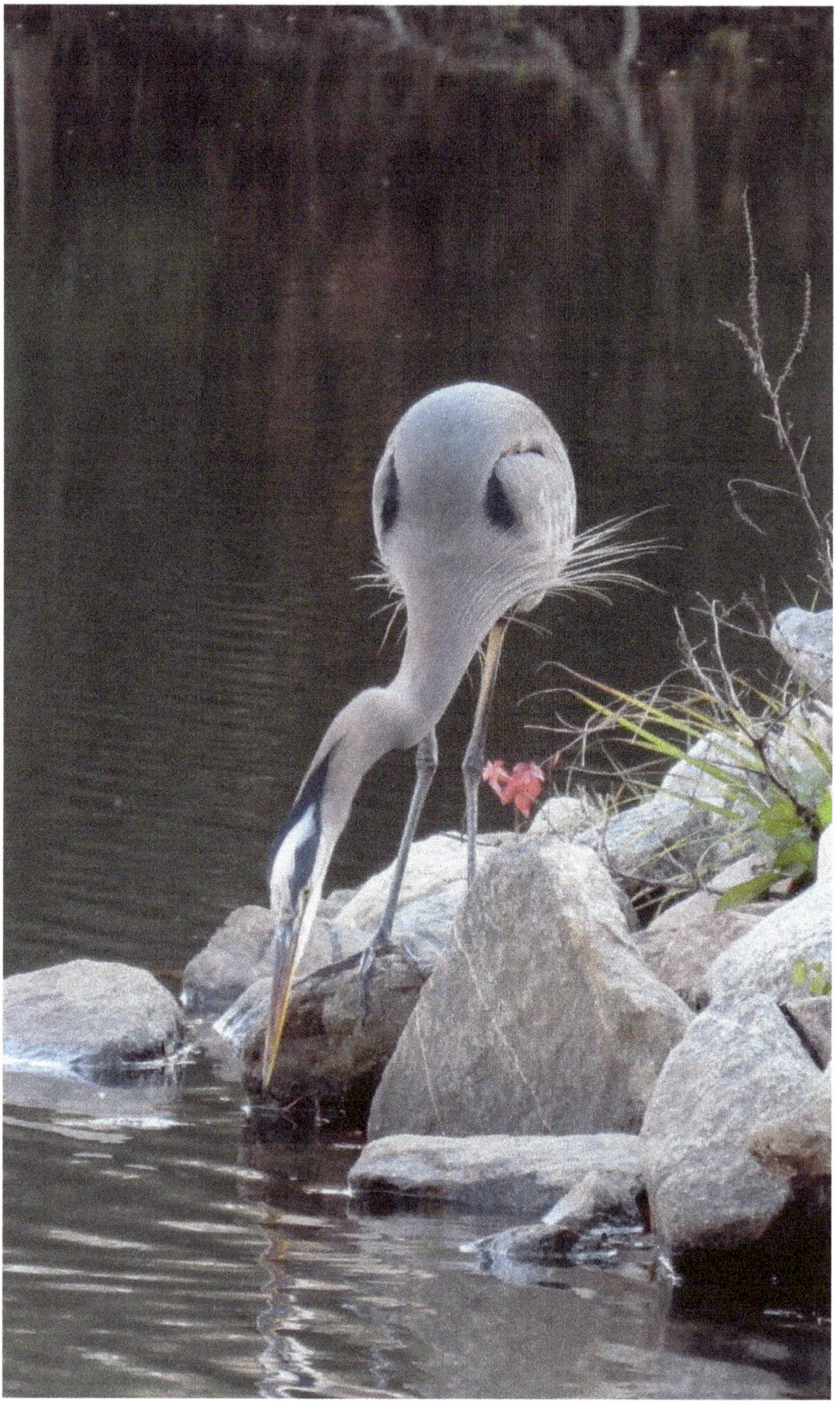

Whatever position you find yourself in, move forward with humility. Personal limits are endless, but afford well intentioned success,

if you simply try.

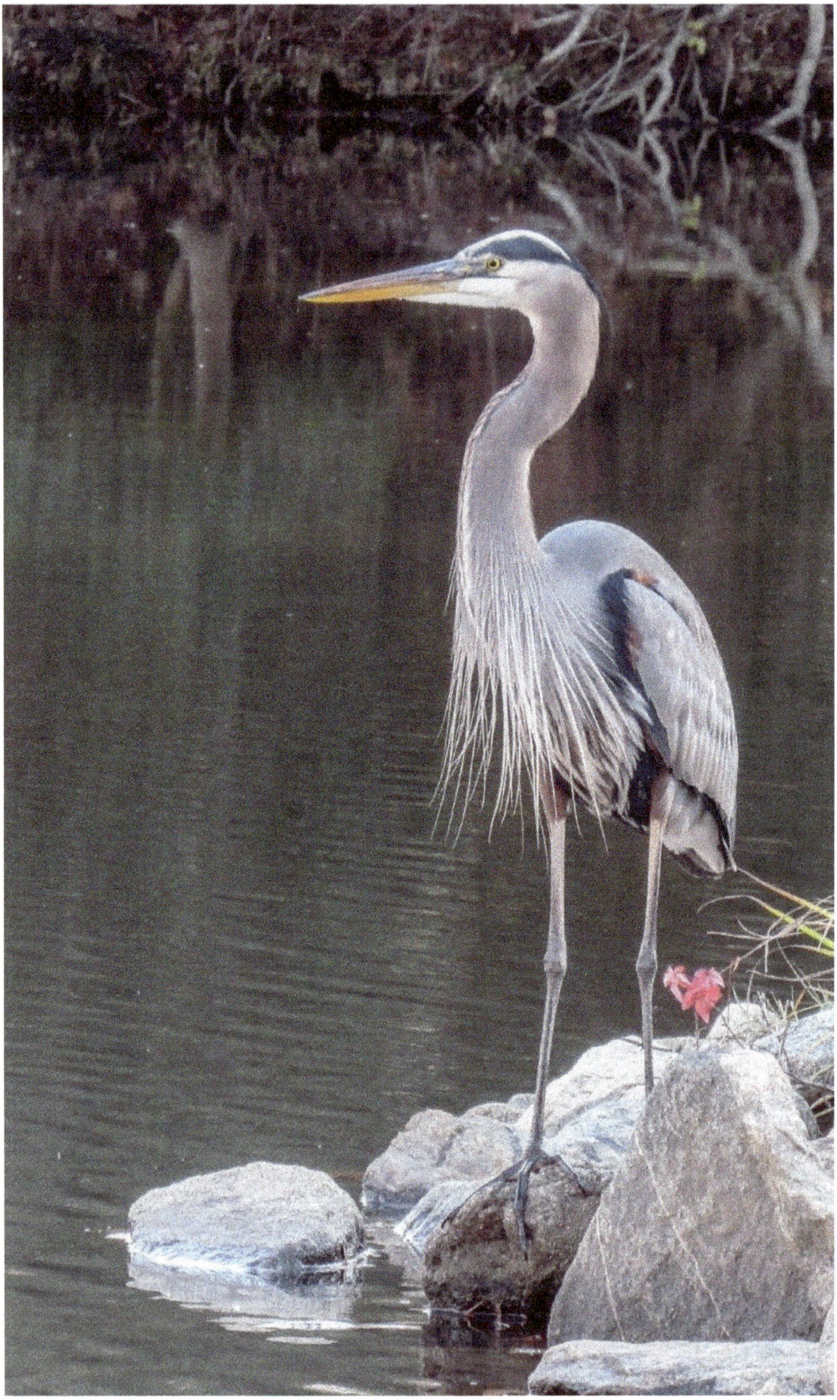

The heart leaf feathers our well-being. Stay warm and amenable for new love surrounds us daily. Simply recognize the expectations of life to give more to others than to receive.

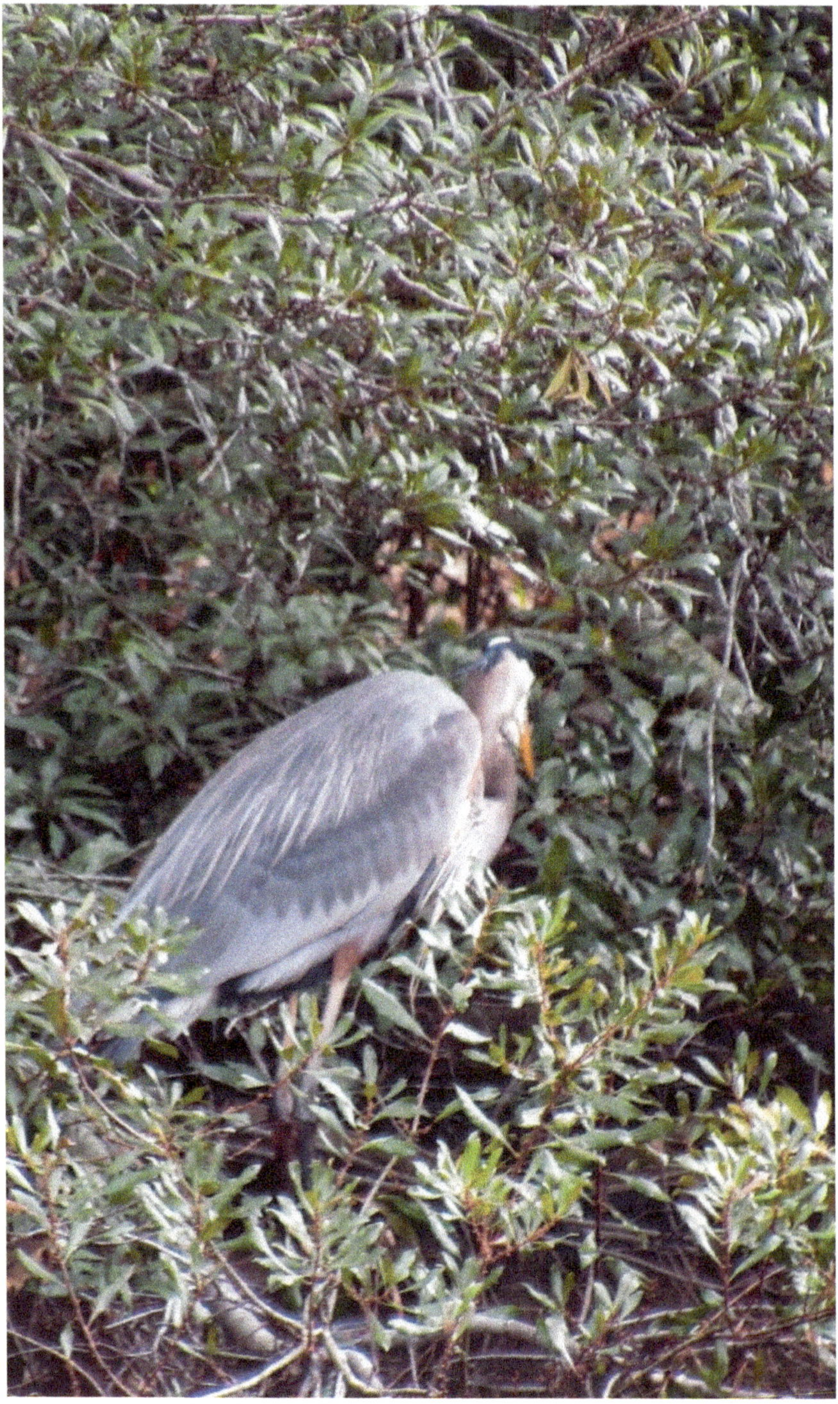

Walk away slowly. Your infinite treasures grow in abundance and will be appreciated day after day and time after time.

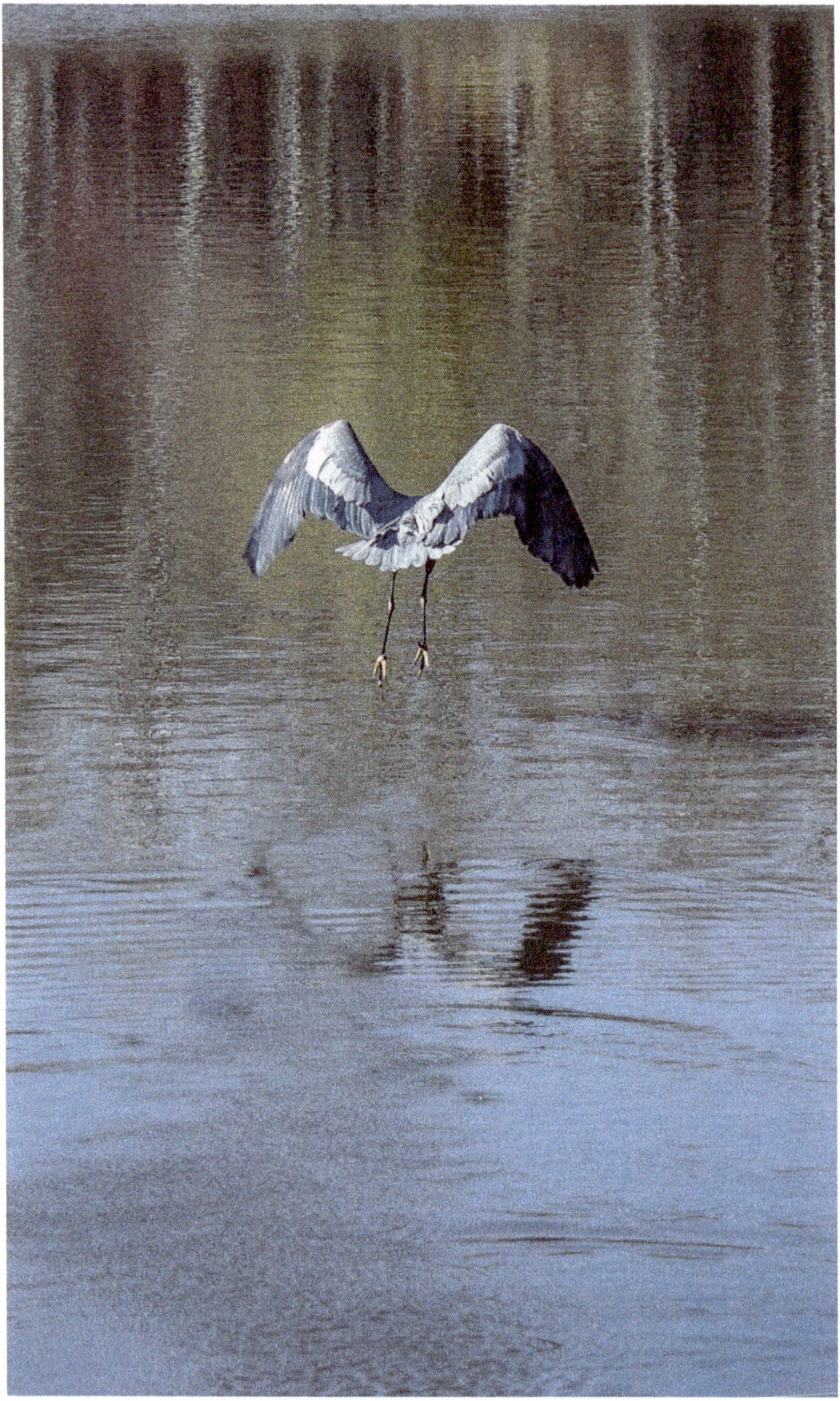

Our determination reflects a passion for life. Be greater than yourself. Windows to the world exist. Soar to the next destination.

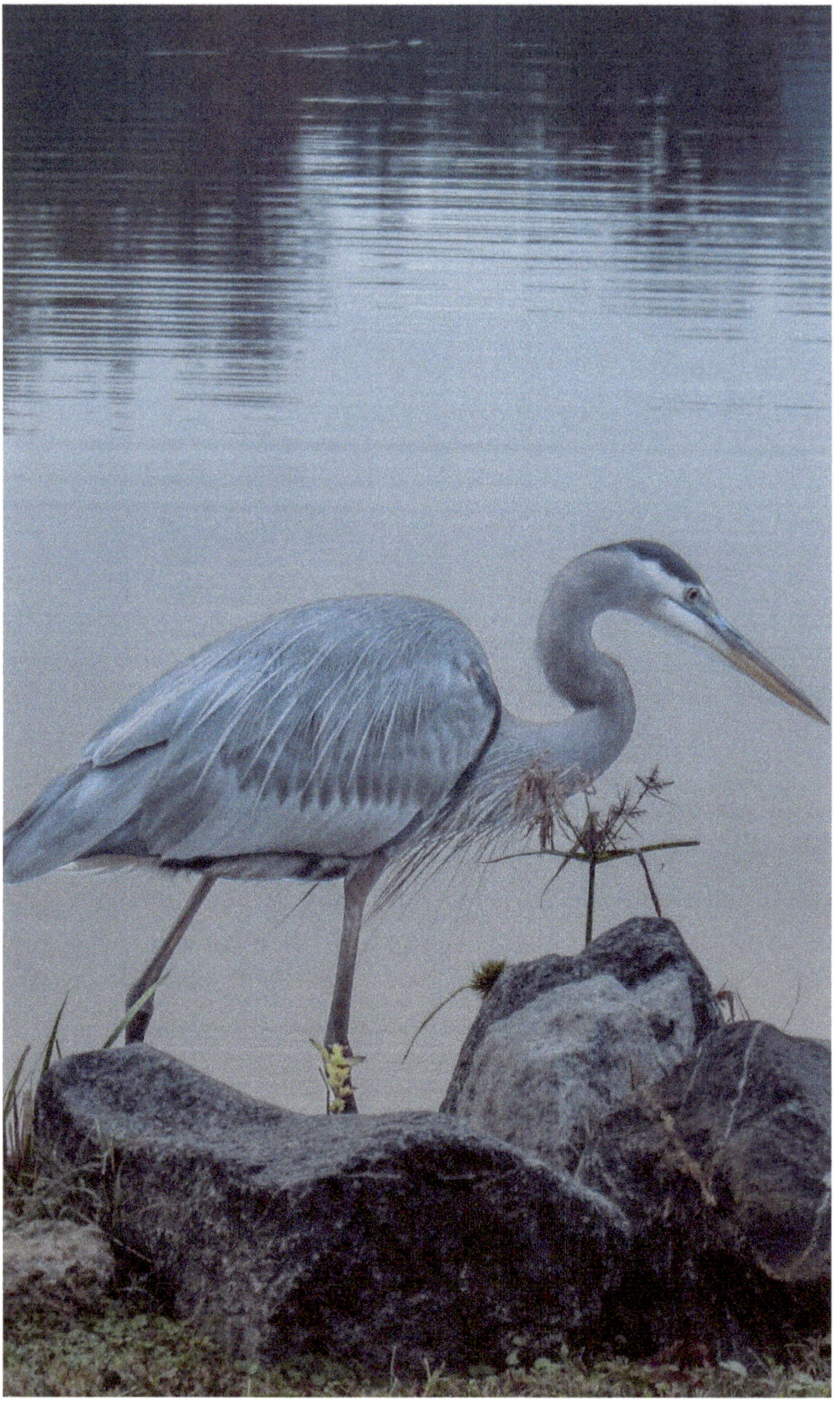

Strength and purpose embrace a new morning. Never shy away from what can be. The enticing rewards will be amazing.

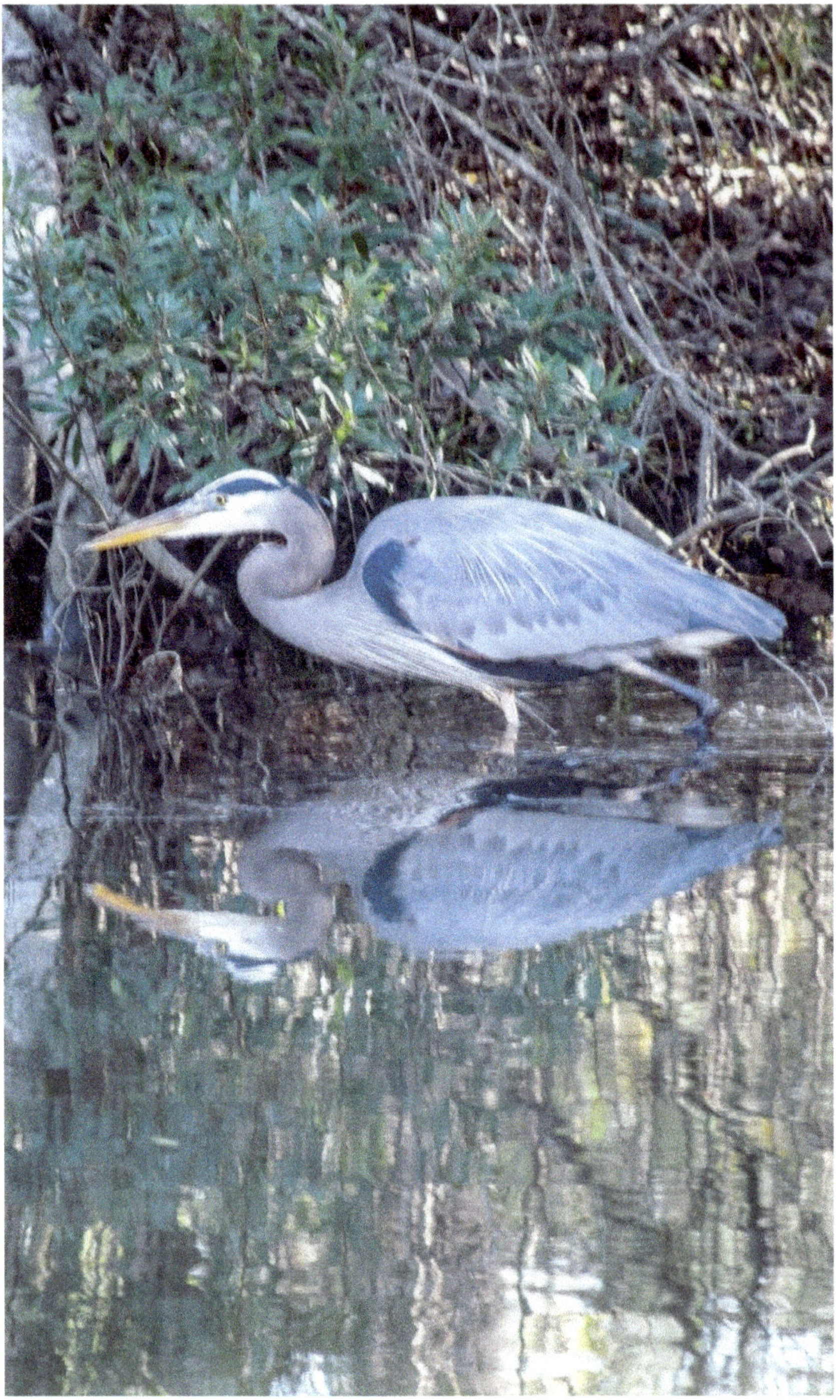

Our fortitude moves us ahead. Never lose sight of what can be your future. Manage an array of choices and determine the course forward wisely.

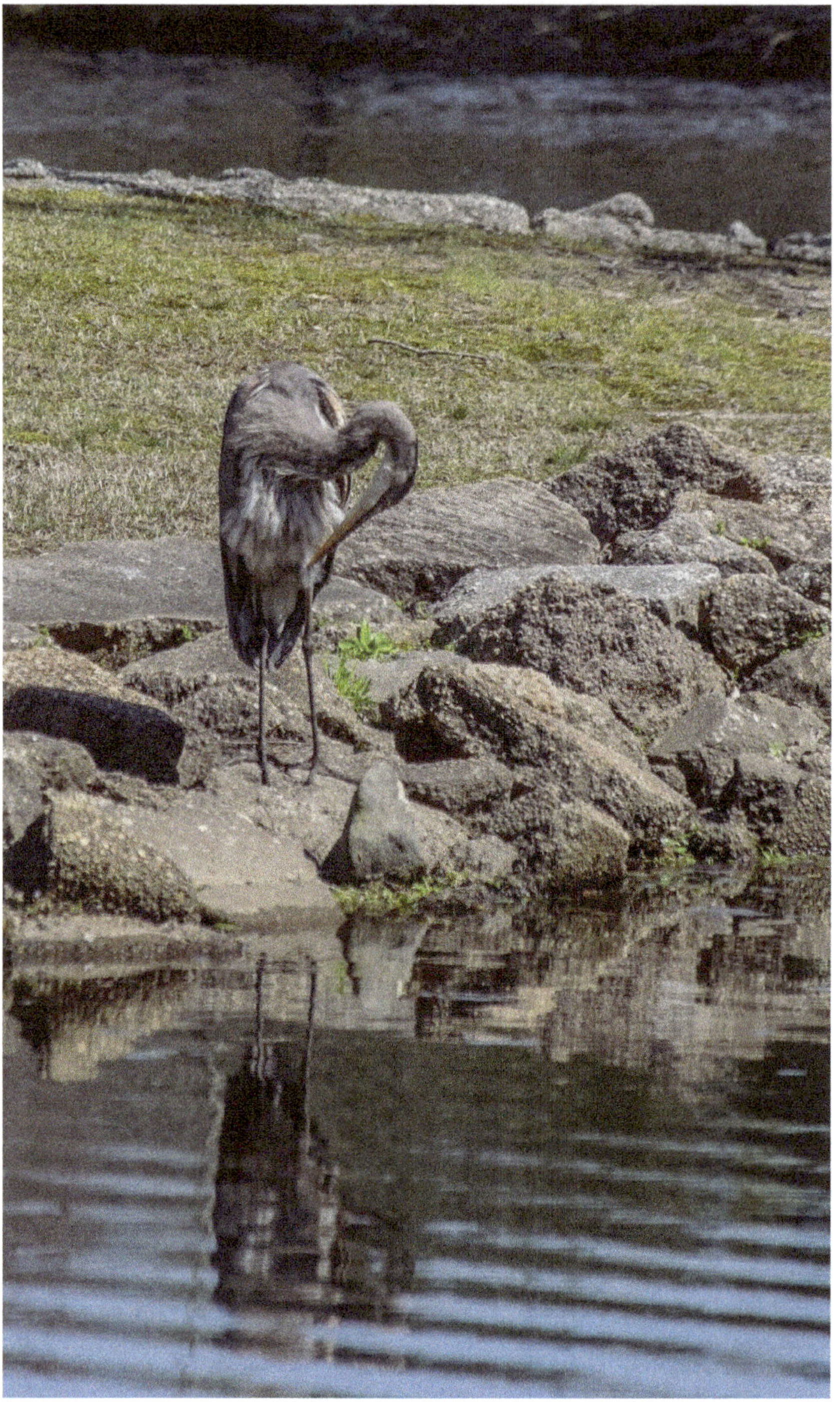

Focus on life. Groom for success. Prepare with precision.

Natural beauty looks stunning on us.

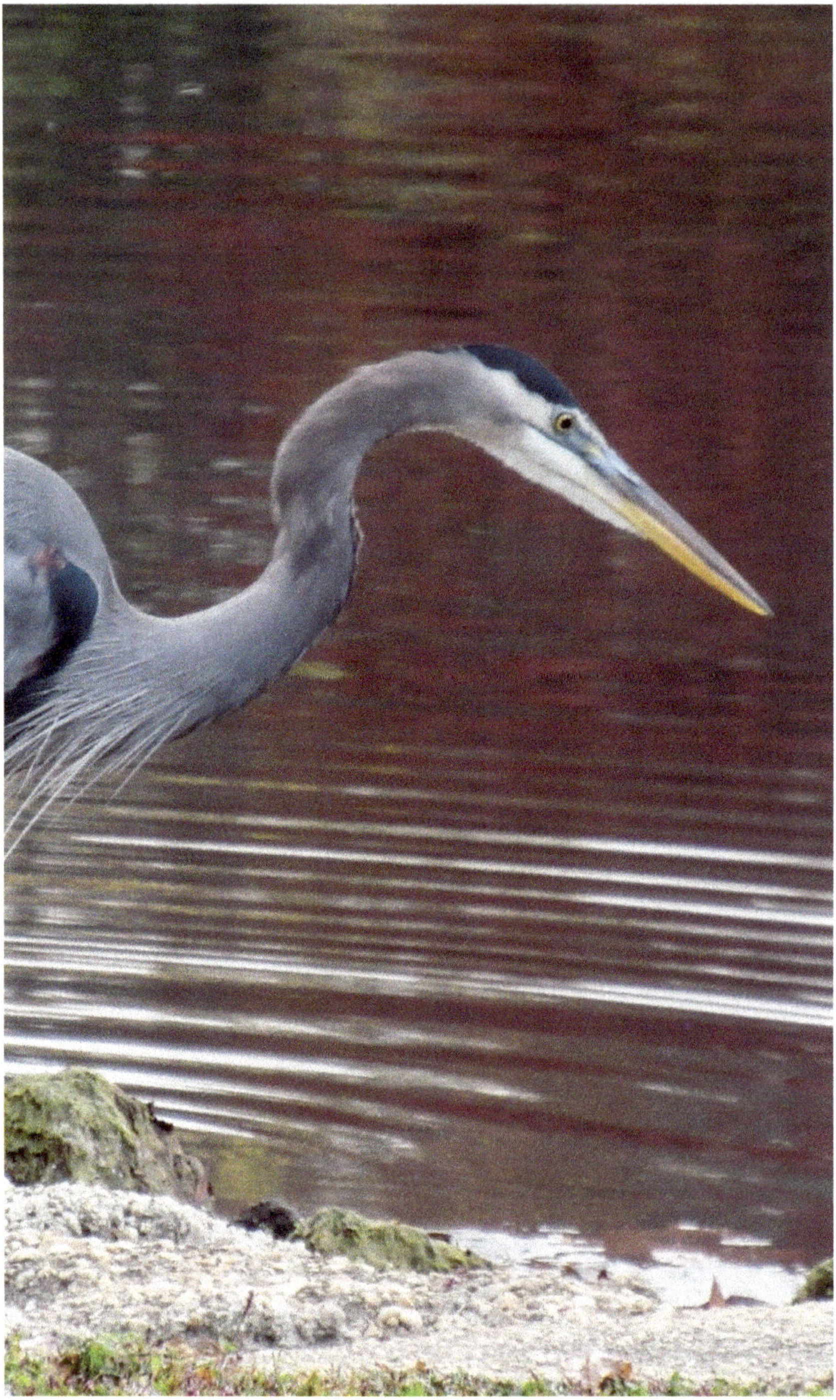

Steady and secure. Life is full of incredible possibilities.

Re-image yourself into positive vitality and resilience.

Shine.

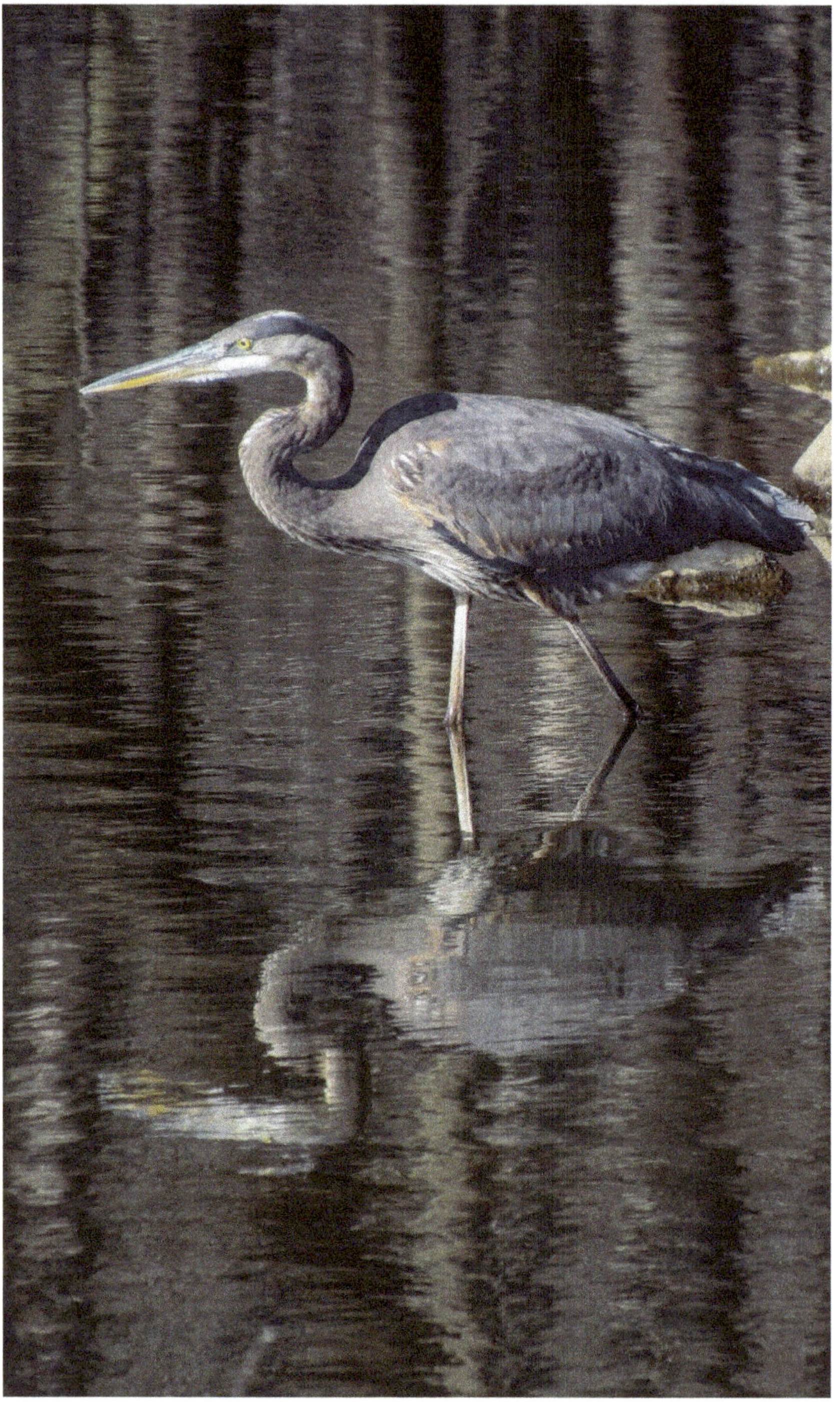

Every aspect of our being is poised to succeed and to thrive. Know no constraints. Today, tomorrow, and always.

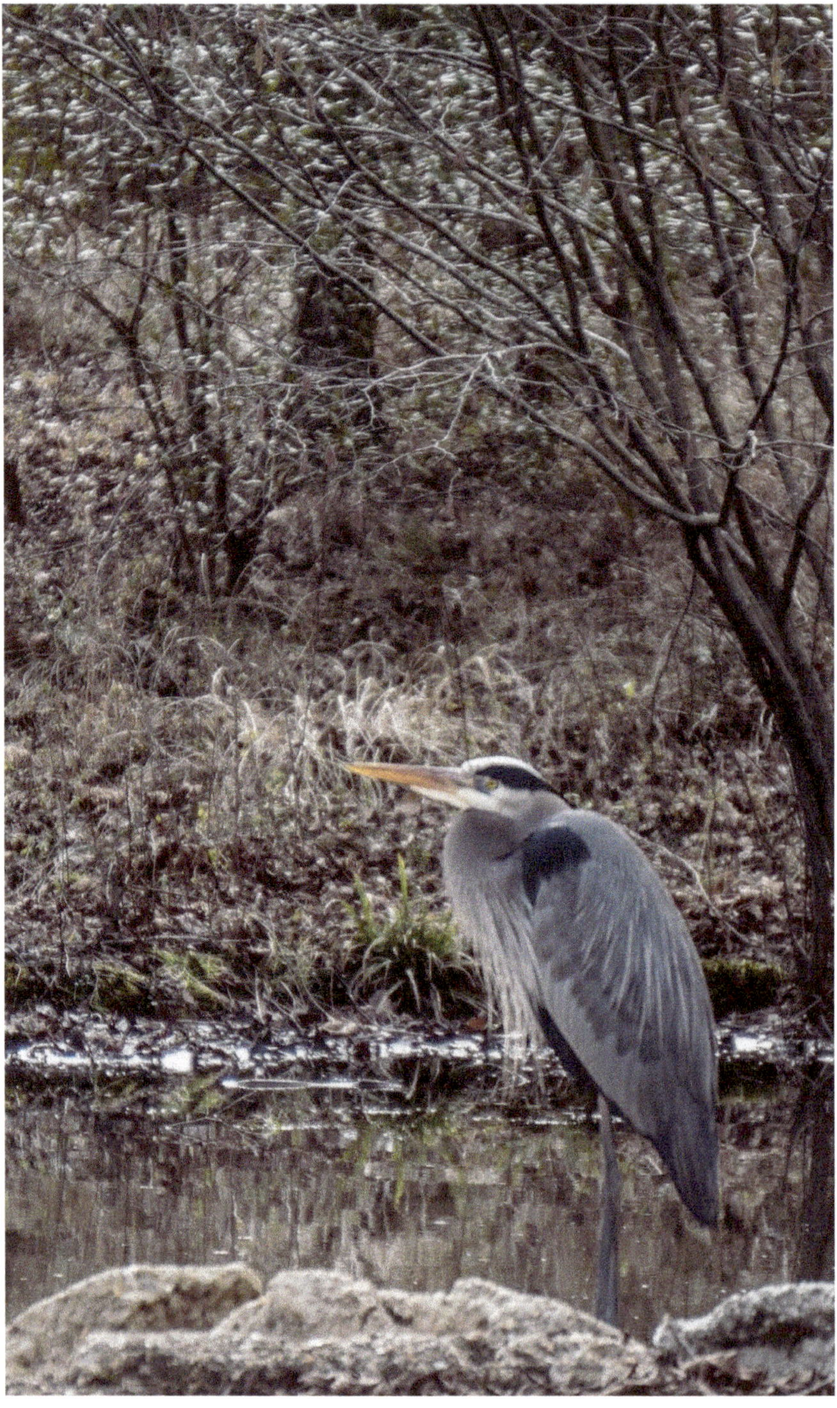

Calm and cool. Willing to see beyond. Good fortune will

follow with patience and persistence.

Enjoy the unknown...

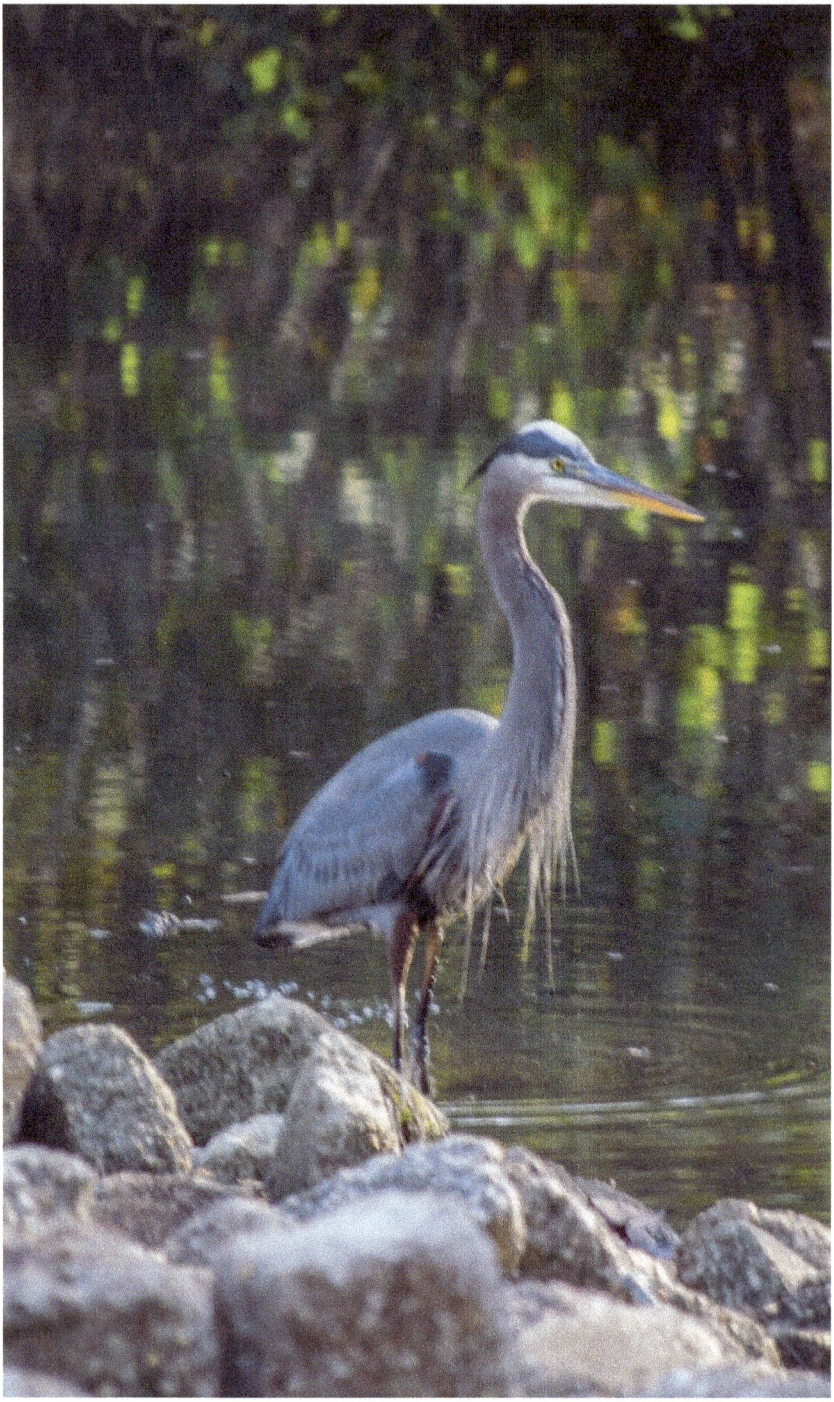

Resourcefulness begins tomorrow. The past becomes the building block of the present. Lean on continued growth to determine your destiny.

Embrace the journey.

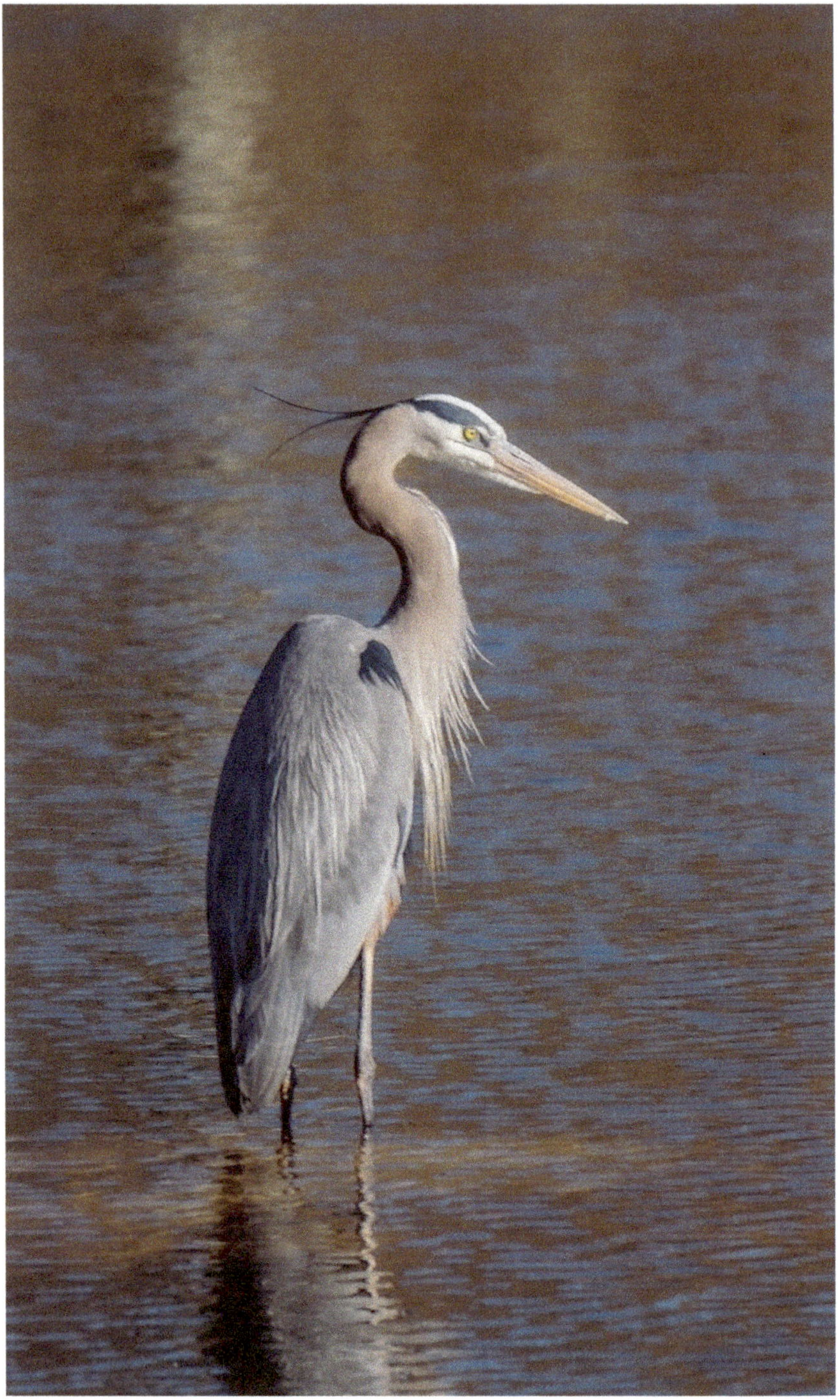

Experience becomes part of a greater creation. The world

is full of sparkling astonishment.

For the beauty of one enhances us all.

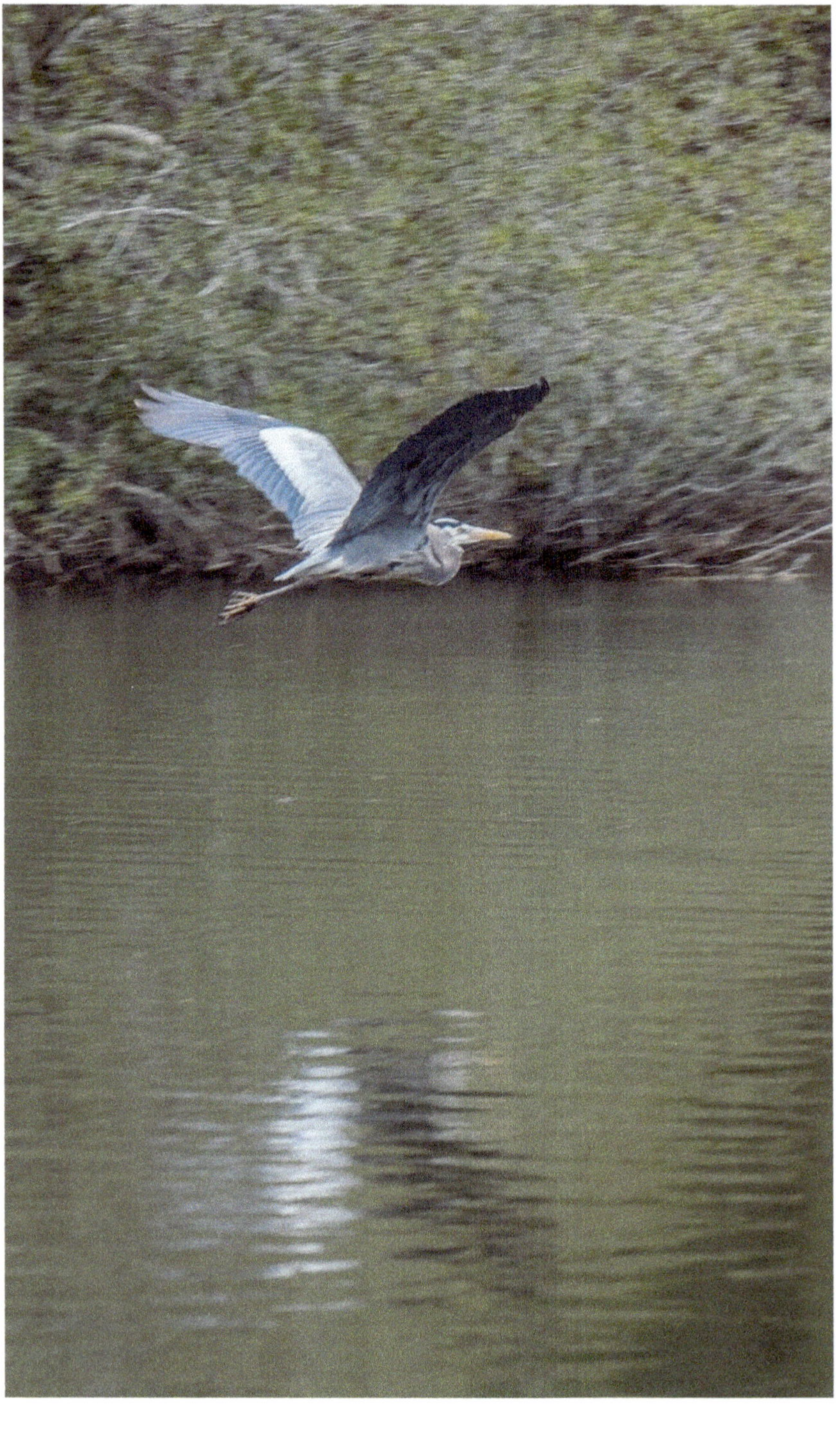

Follow closely and take wing. You will be thrust high into the future and within sight of your dreams.

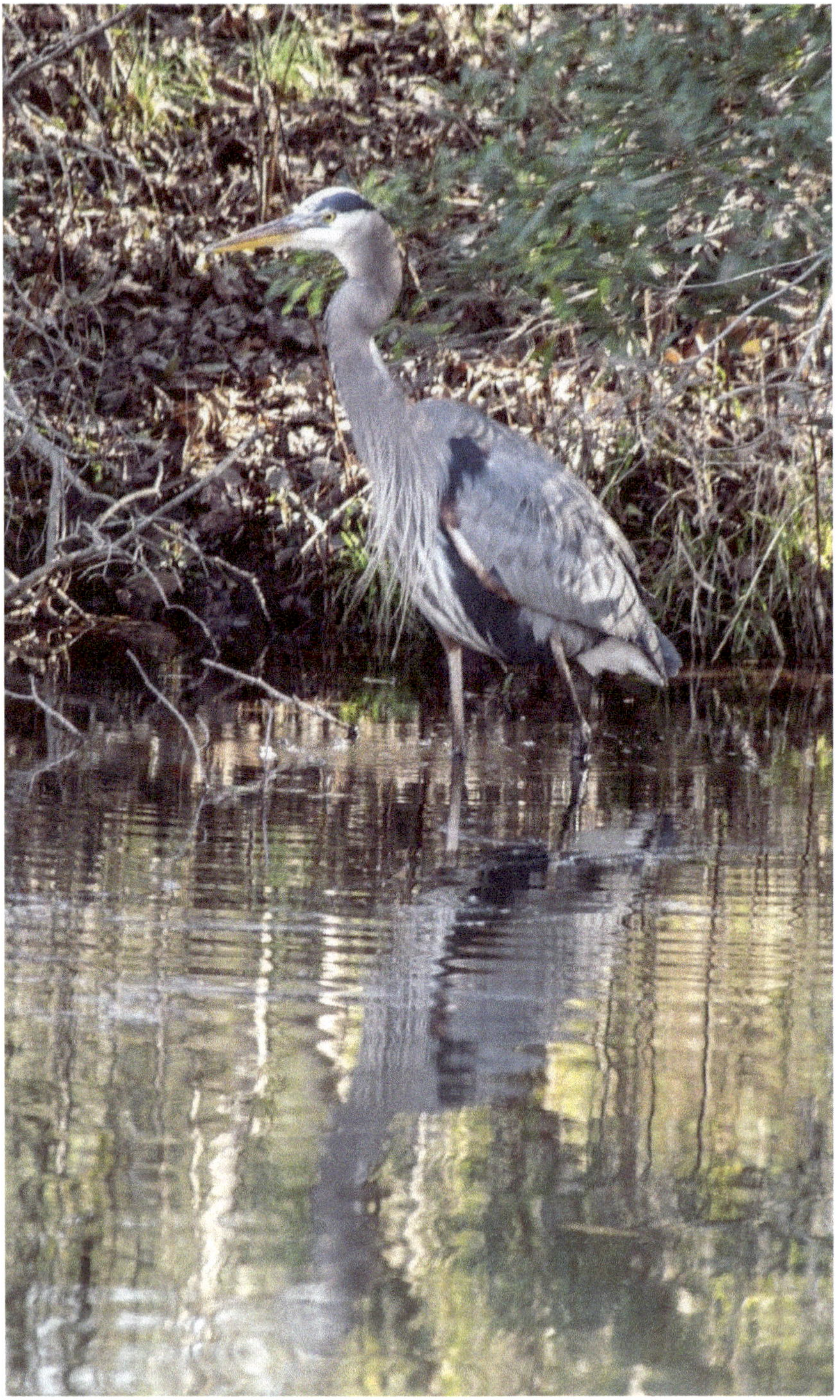

It is our philosophical nature to view life completely. With each moment comes a new realization to build upon yesterday and make it remarkable.

Life unfolds.

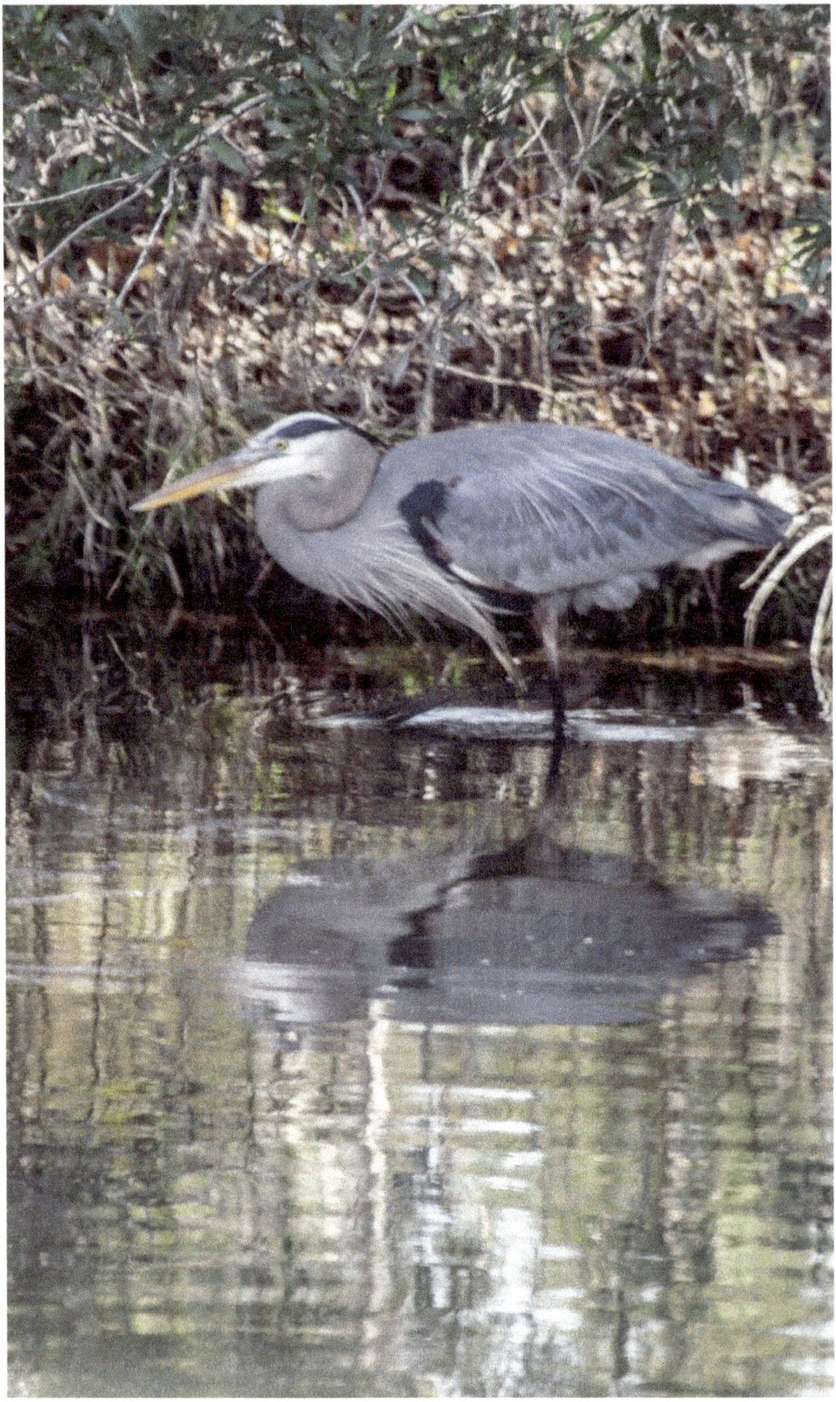

Shadows of blue provide cover in the water, in the sky, and in our surroundings. Blessed to be a small, but an integral part of existence.

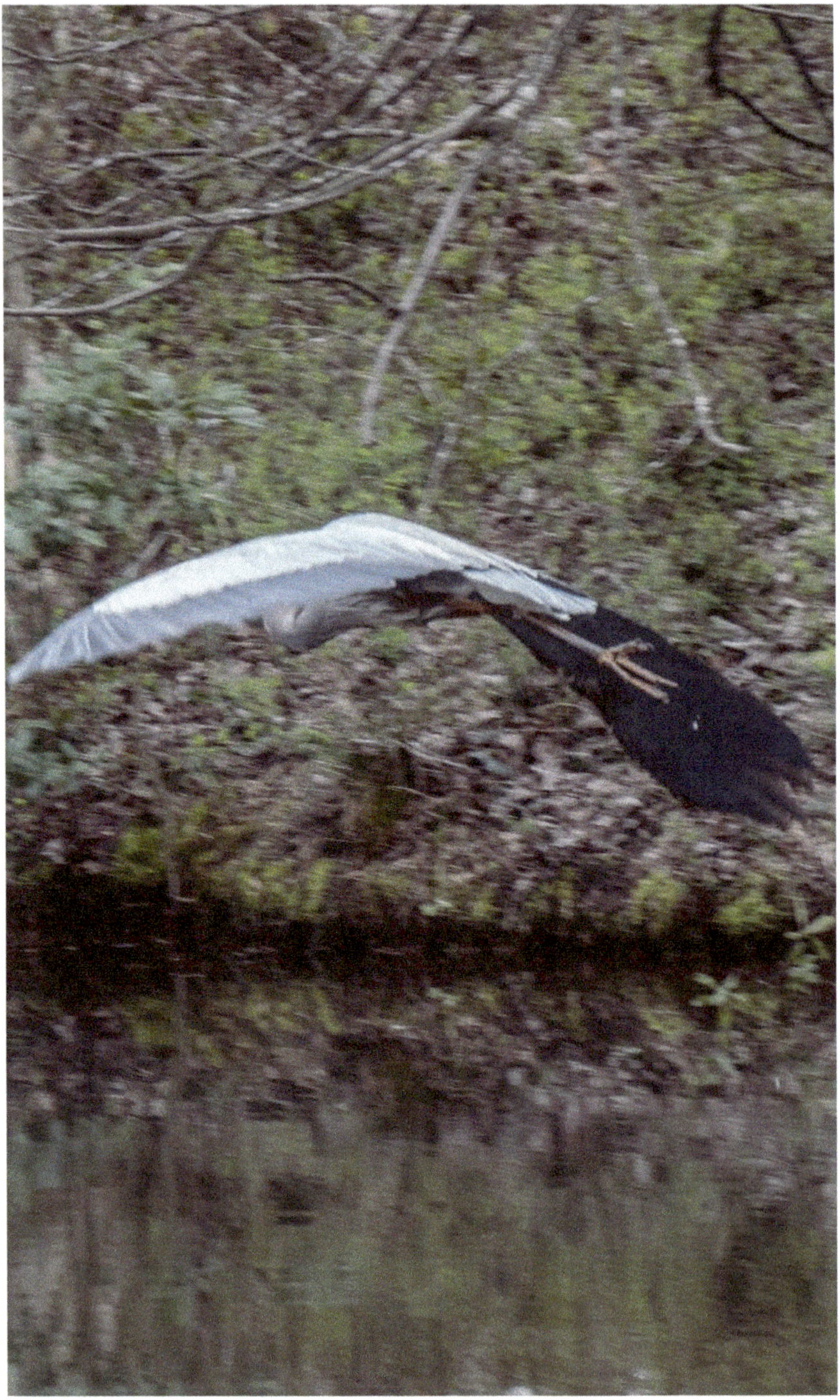

Sending thoughts for what lies ahead. The warmth of your being will tingle with excitement and laughter. Destiny nears with expectation.

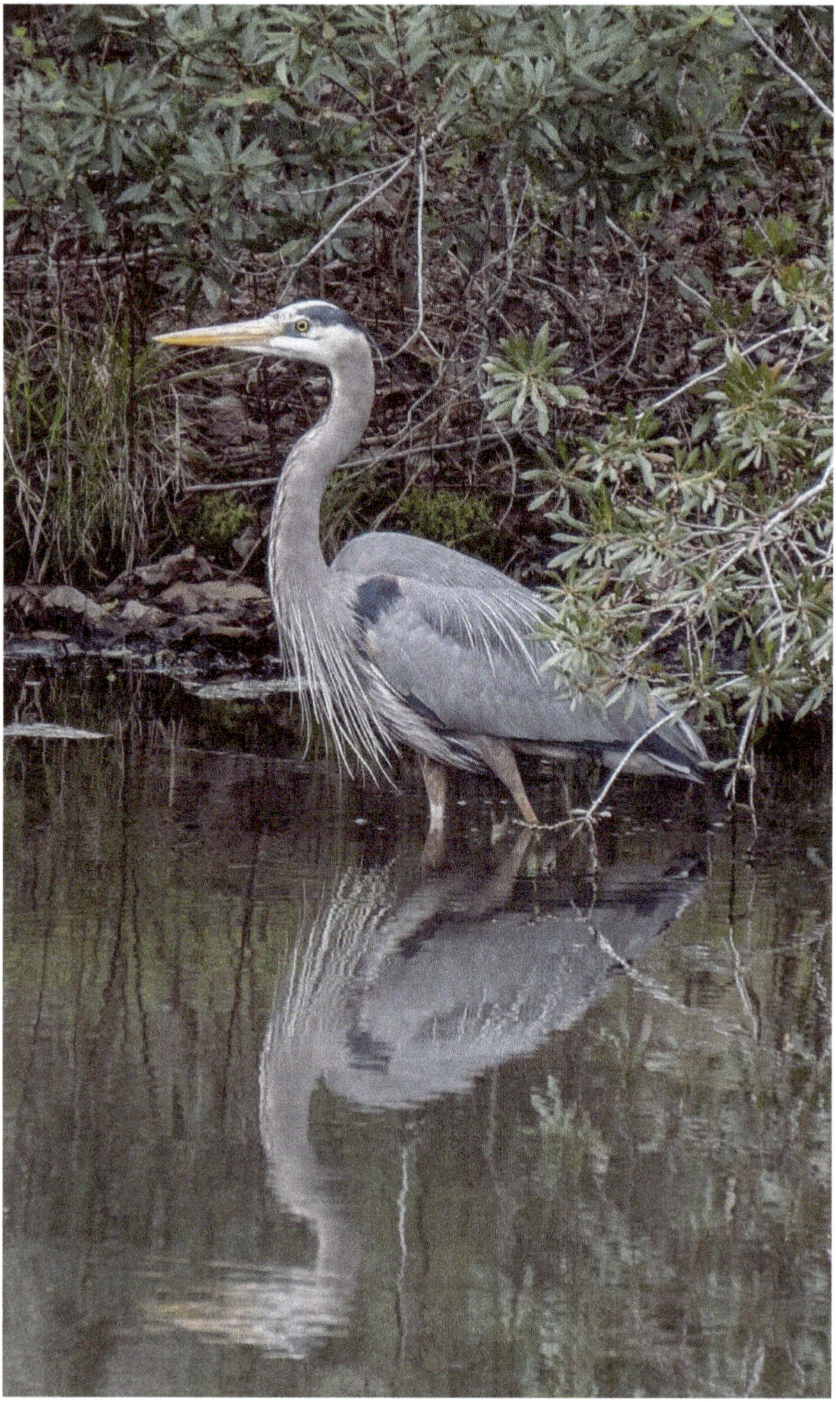

Reflections are reminders of who we are. Never stand alone. Know that you are cherished.

Forever.

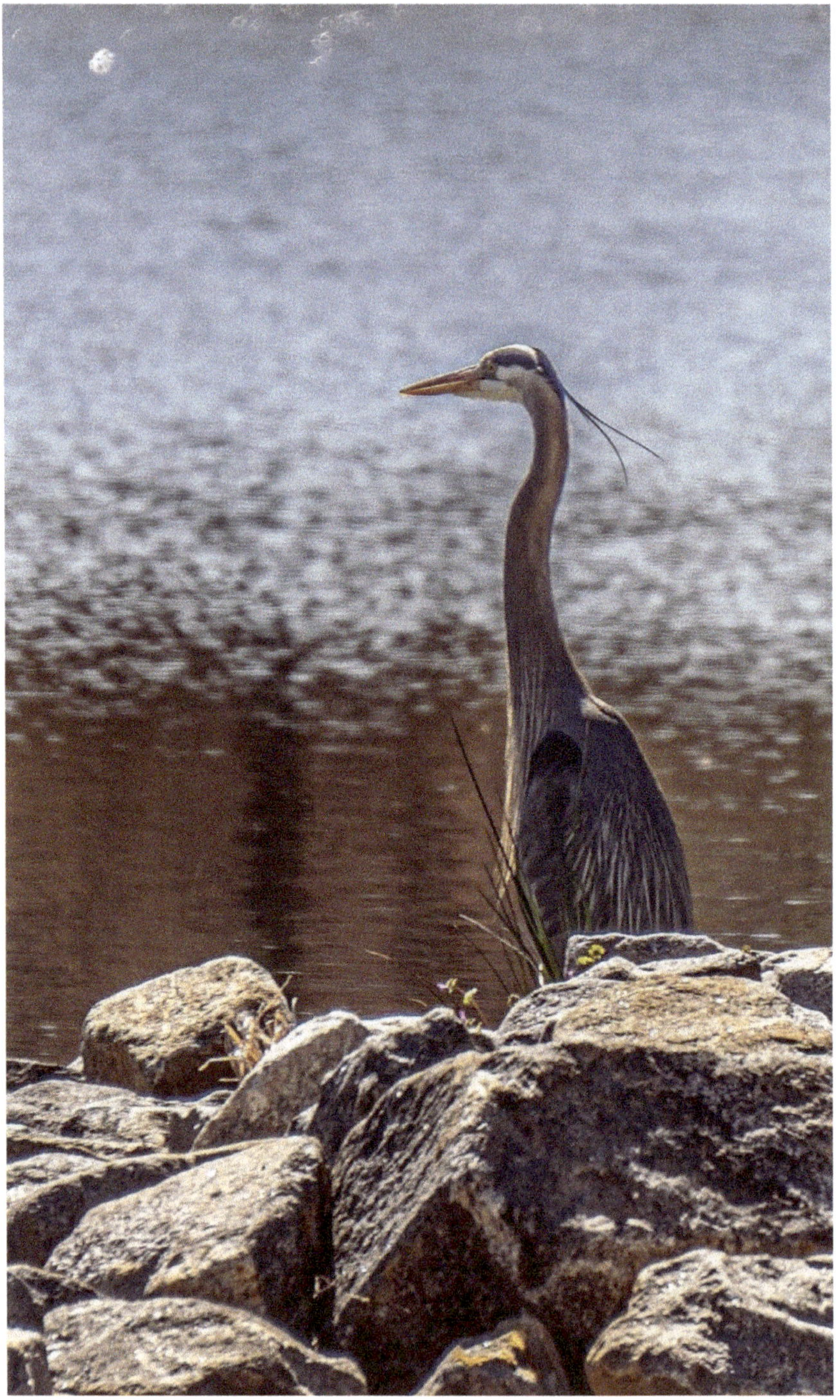

Our prominence is only made greater with a keen sense of mind and soul.

Unfold your talents deep within and stay the course.

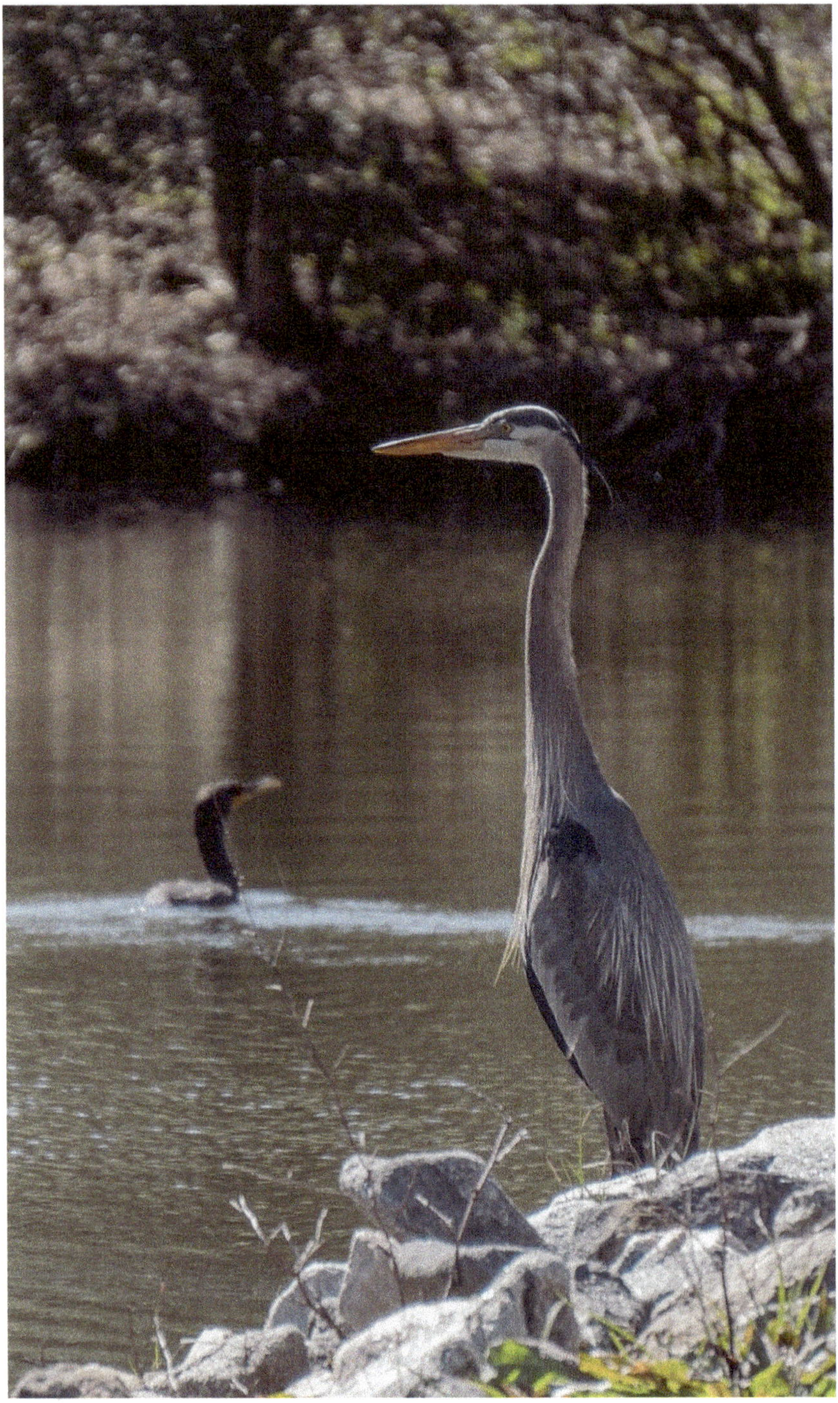

The ripples of life reflect our compassion. Never abandoned, but forever standing ready to simply be recognized by others.

Extraordinary . . .

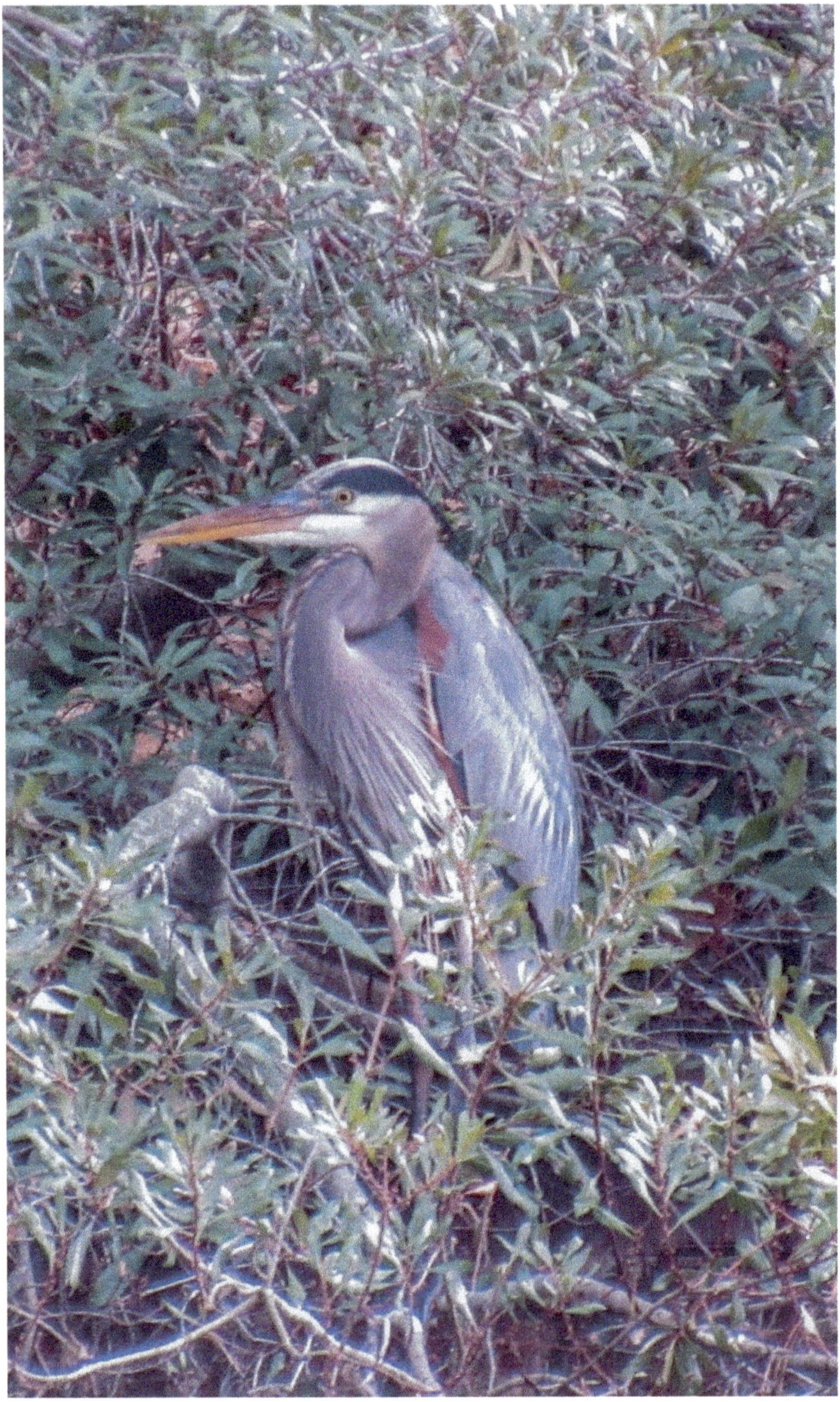

You are complete. Live life to the fullest. Never take your role for granted. We are only limited by time and a reluctance to succeed.

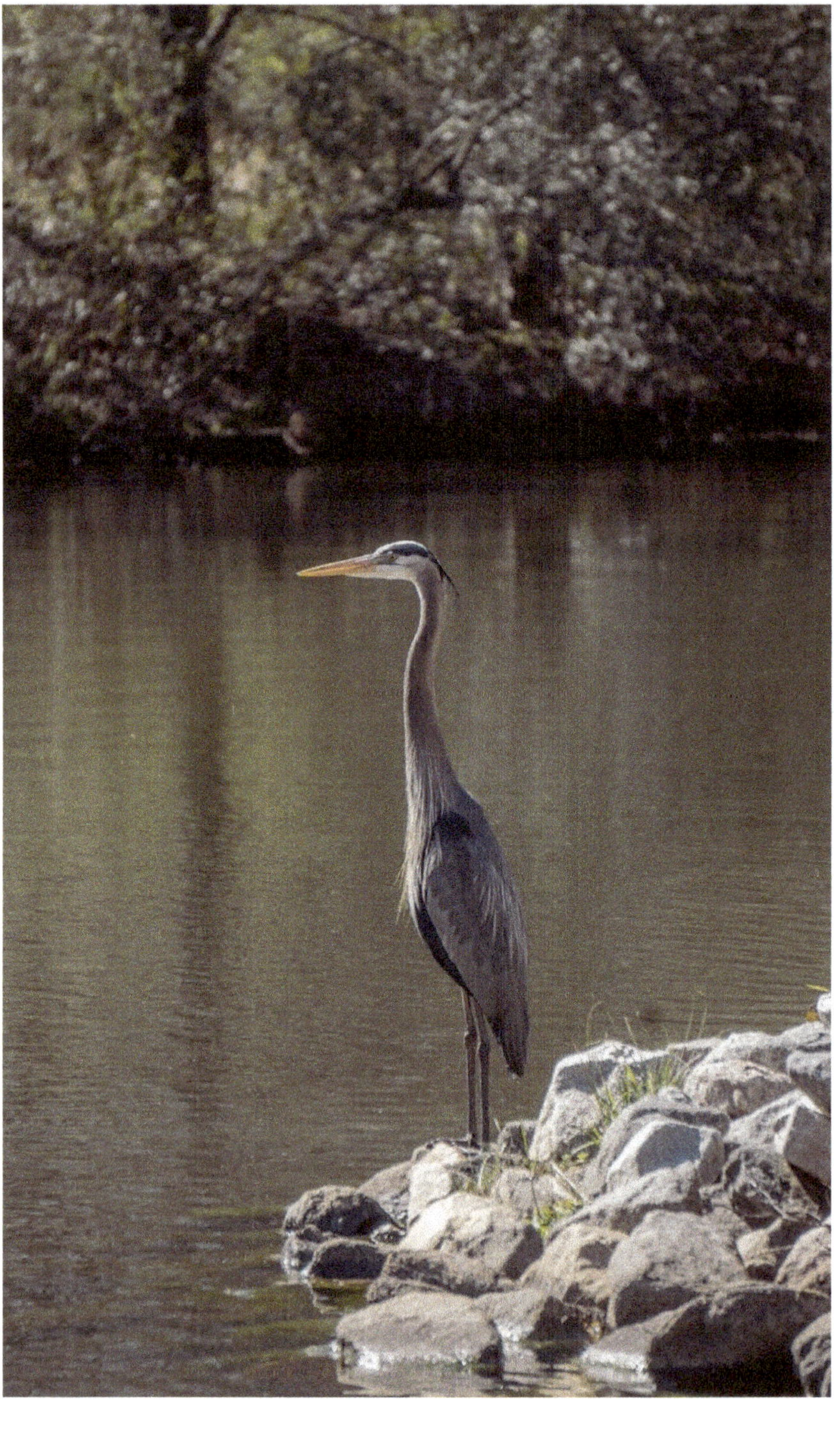

Alert and watchful with the sights and sounds of beauty in our reach. We are one with nature.

Wonderful!

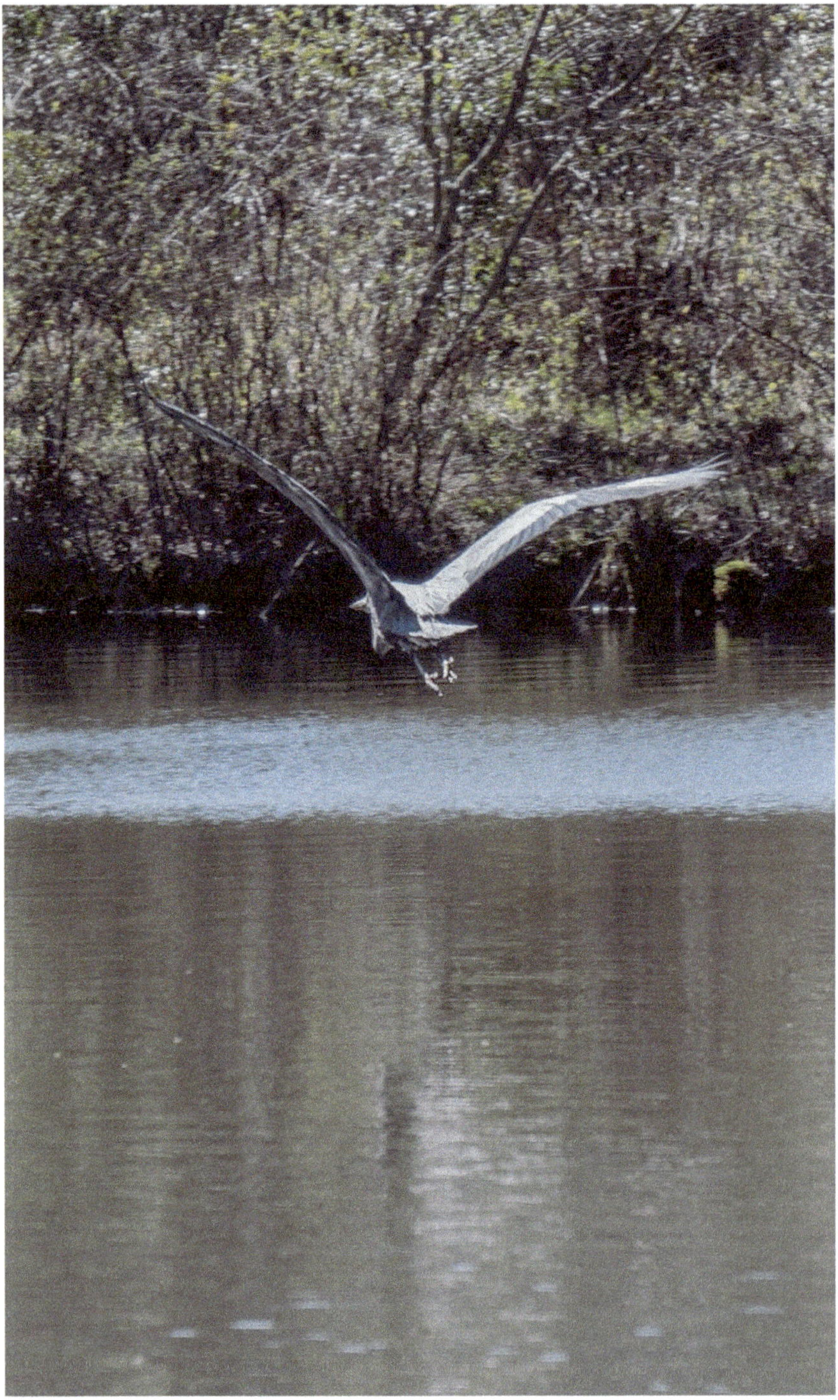

The lake sustains our presence. Be confident in your decisions and make your life choices productive and meaningful.

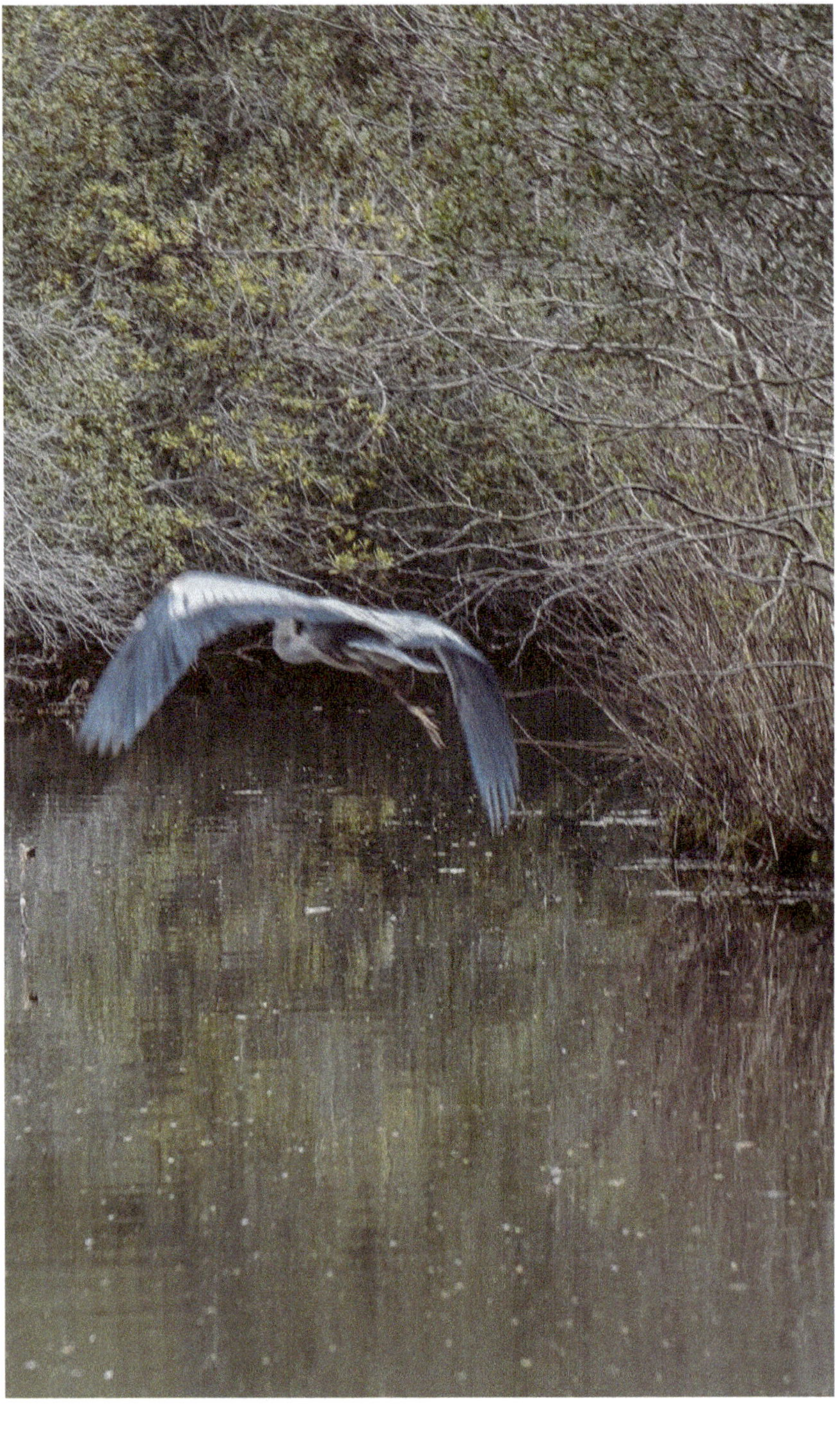

On target to reach our ambitions. Stay with me for

greatness lies around the corner of life.

The wind feels soothing beneath our spirit.

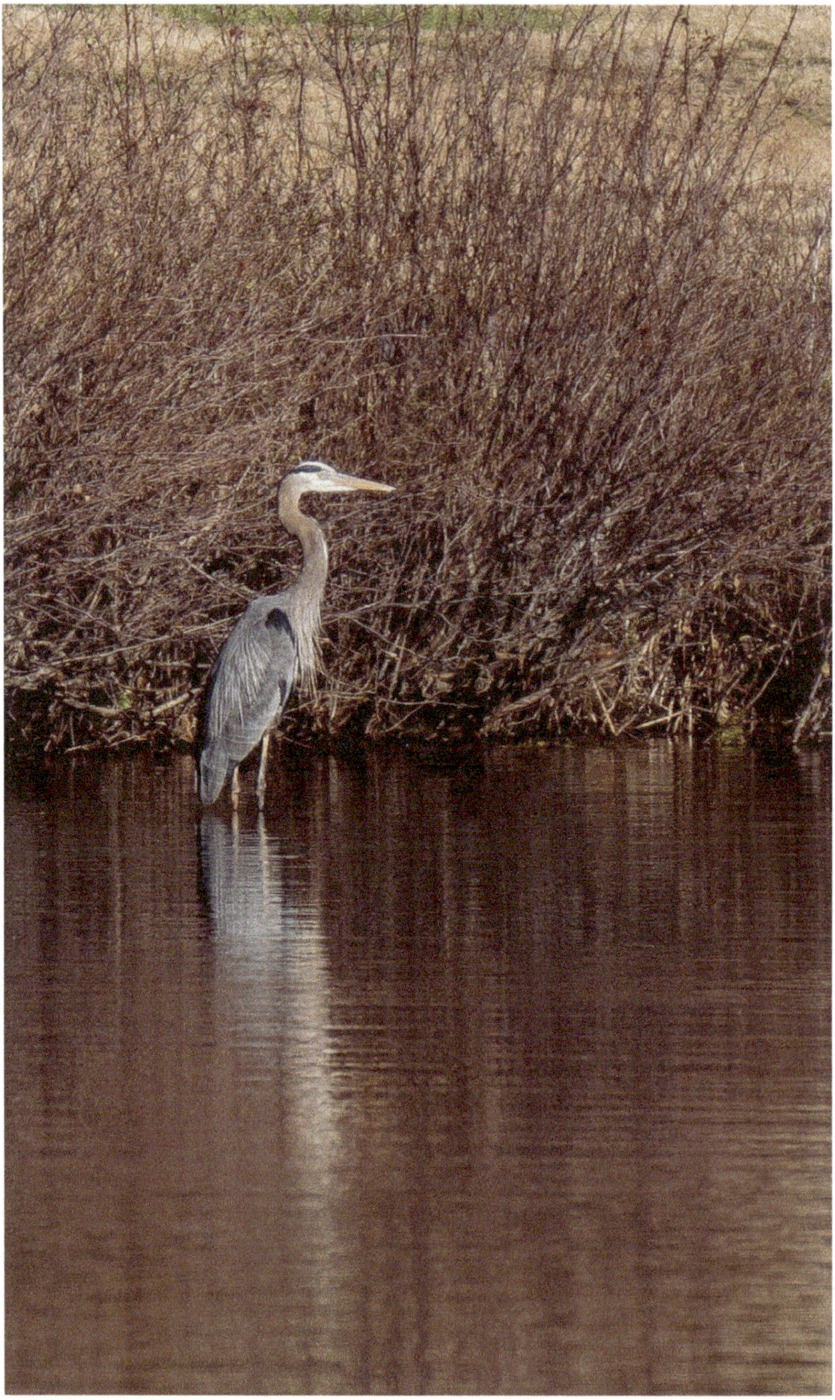

All is visualized in our minds. Share your ideas and make

new paths. Be magnanimous.

The day is golden.

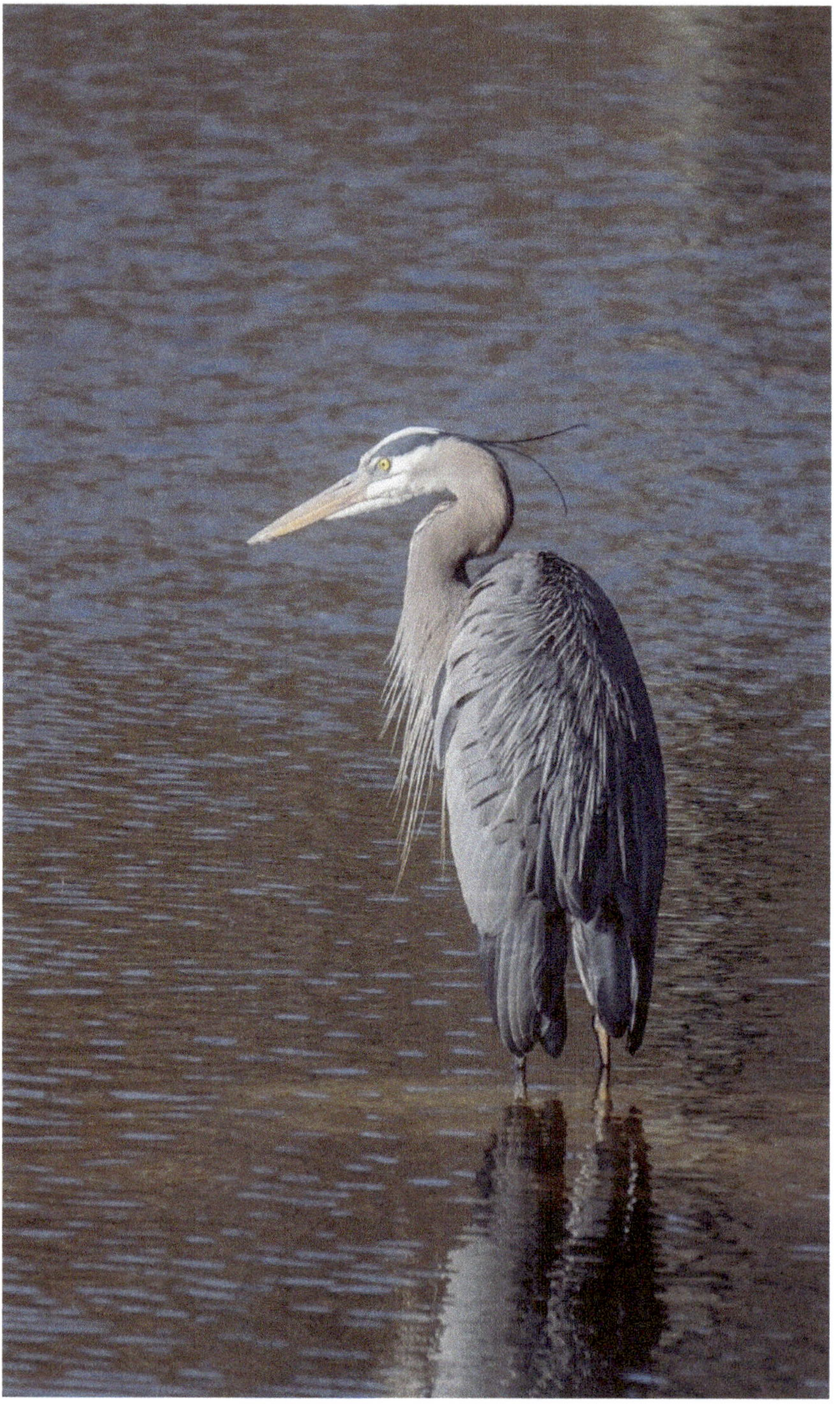

Determination moves us ahead. Never lose sight of what can be your future. Select your choices and thrive.

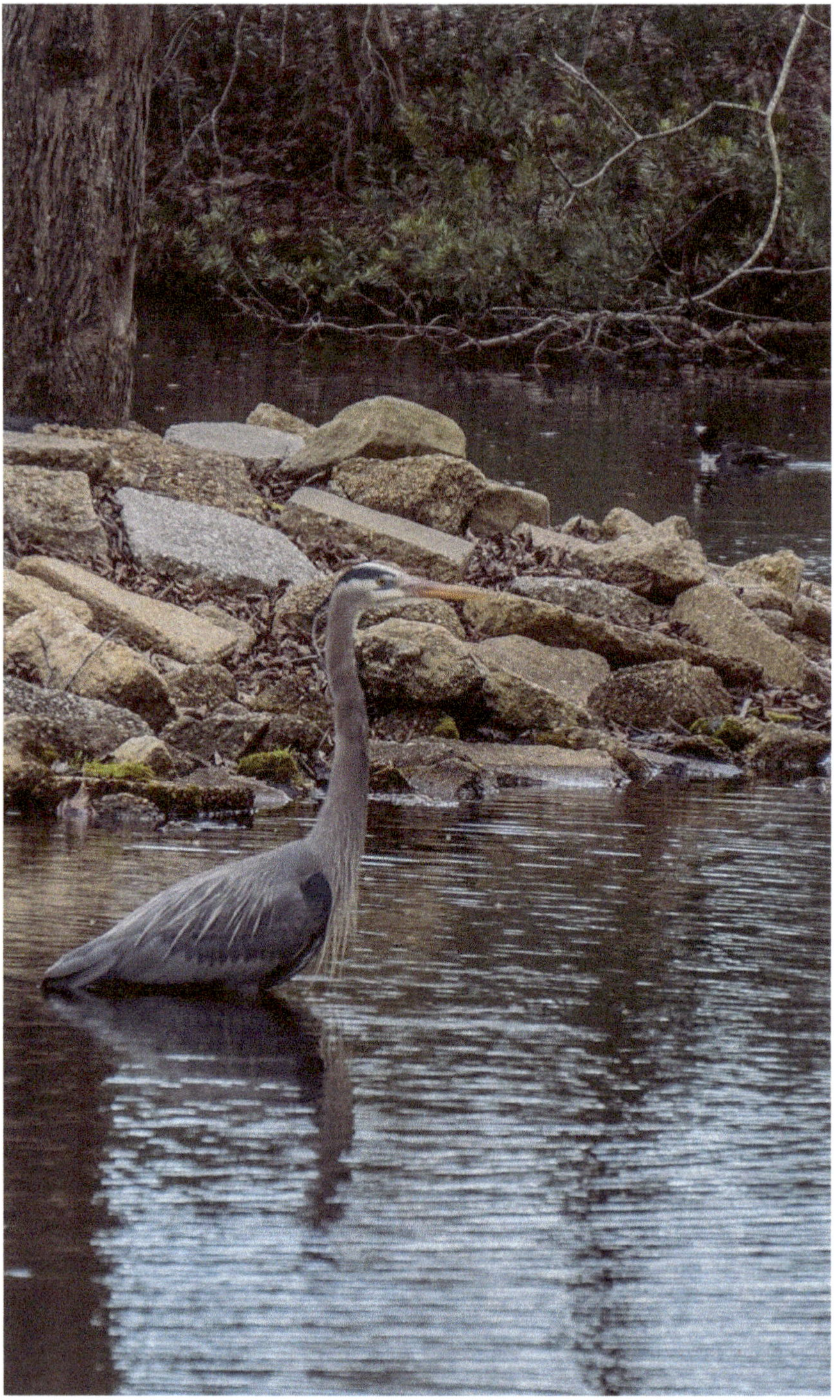

The water compels our thoughts to wander and our being to be satisfied. No day is complete without the next.

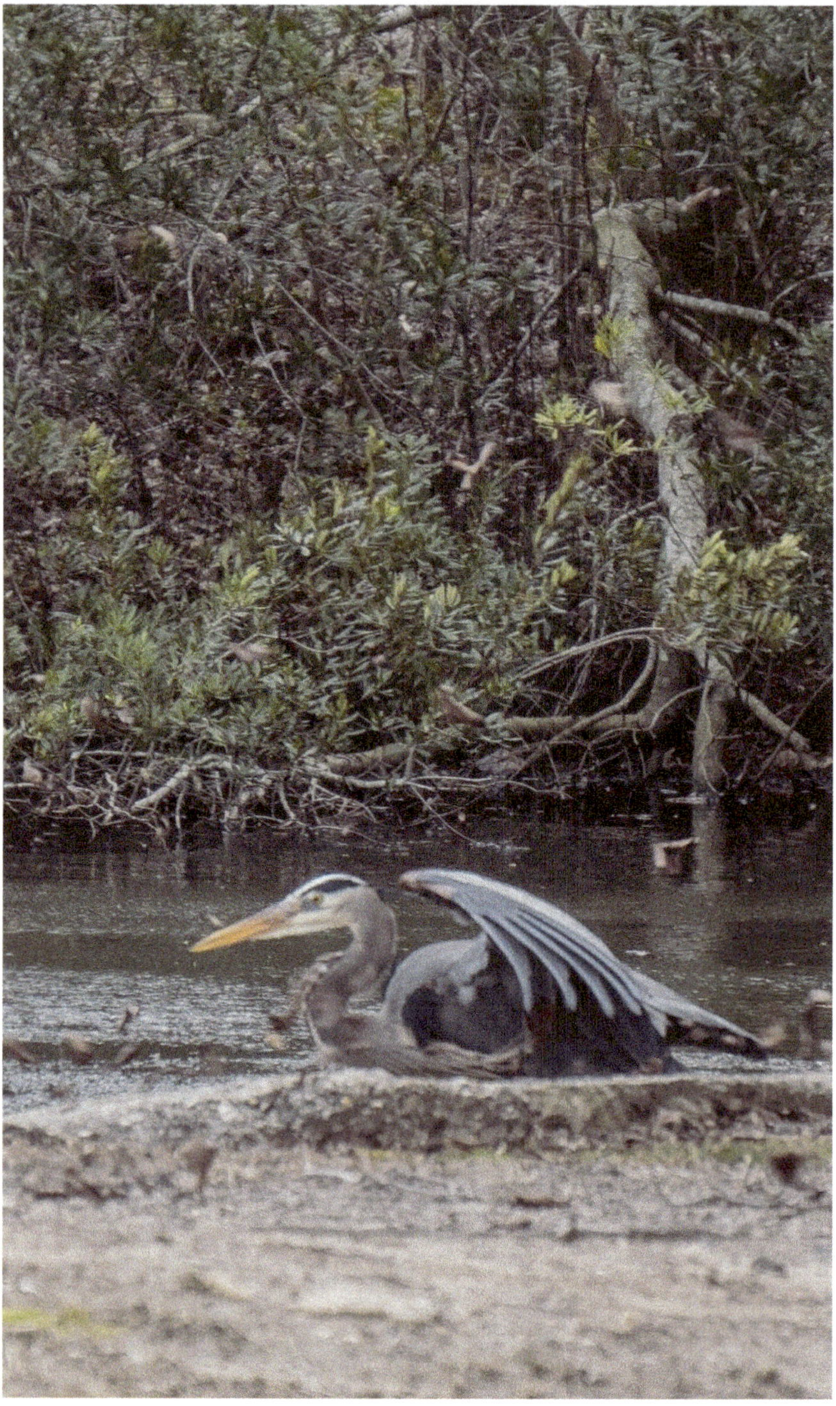

Stay close, precious friend. Moments like these are rare.

Treasure the challenge of simply being you on a beautiful

day.

Enjoy life.

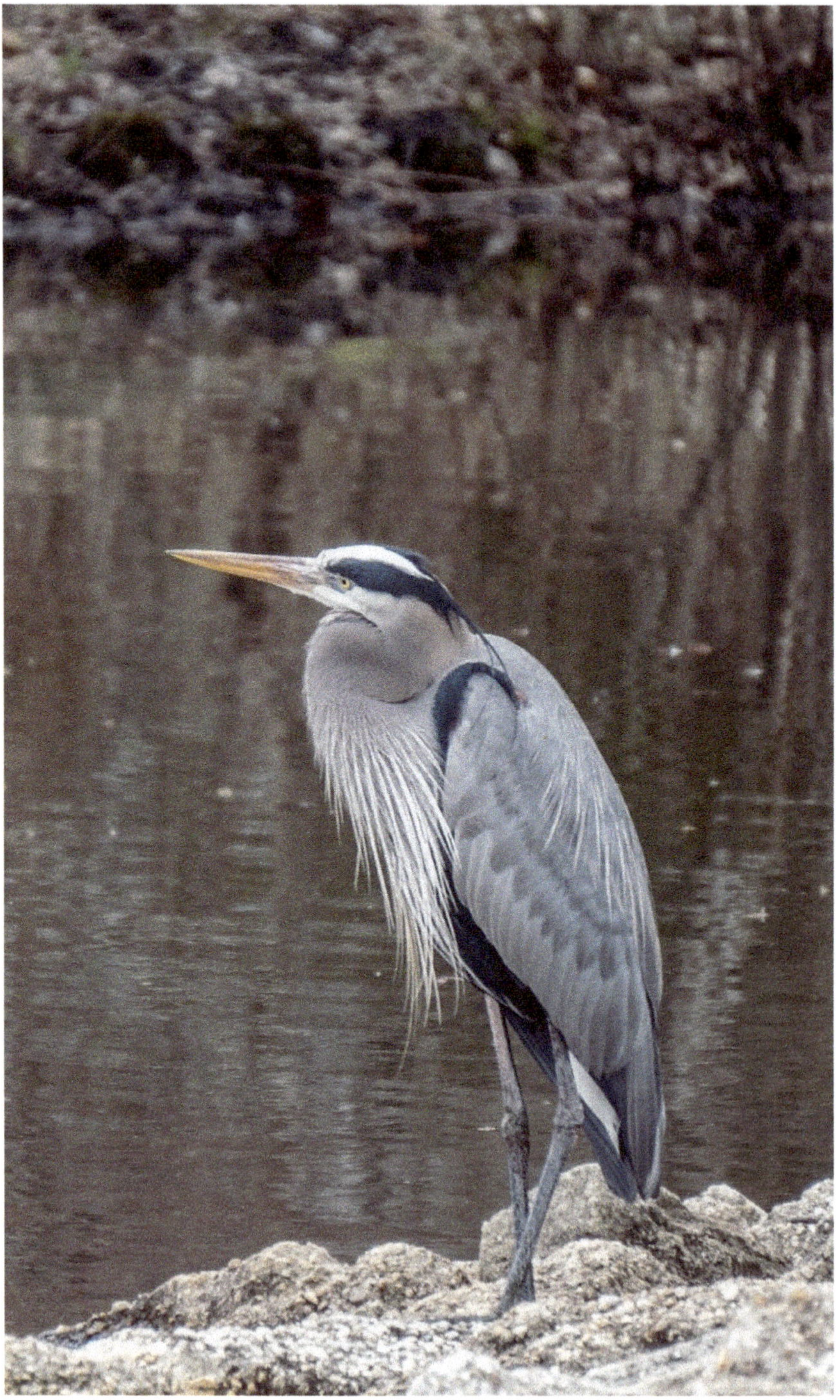

See us for who we are. Bold, beautiful, and filled with powerful instincts within. With a tilt of the head, lead and follow with determination and insight.

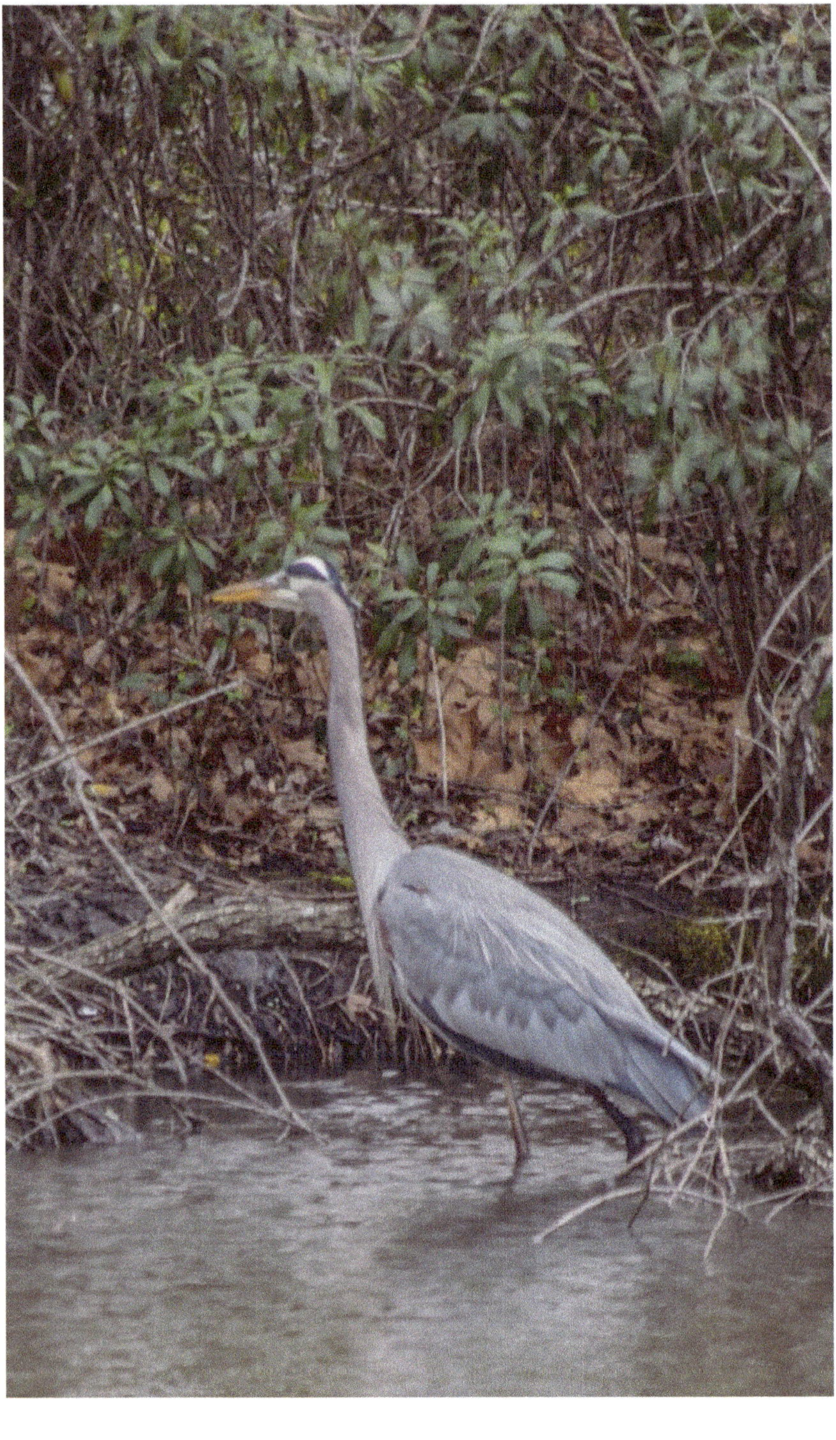

Enough for all. Share the journey with a strong desire to realize the pinnacle of your existence.

Live long and be true to yourself.

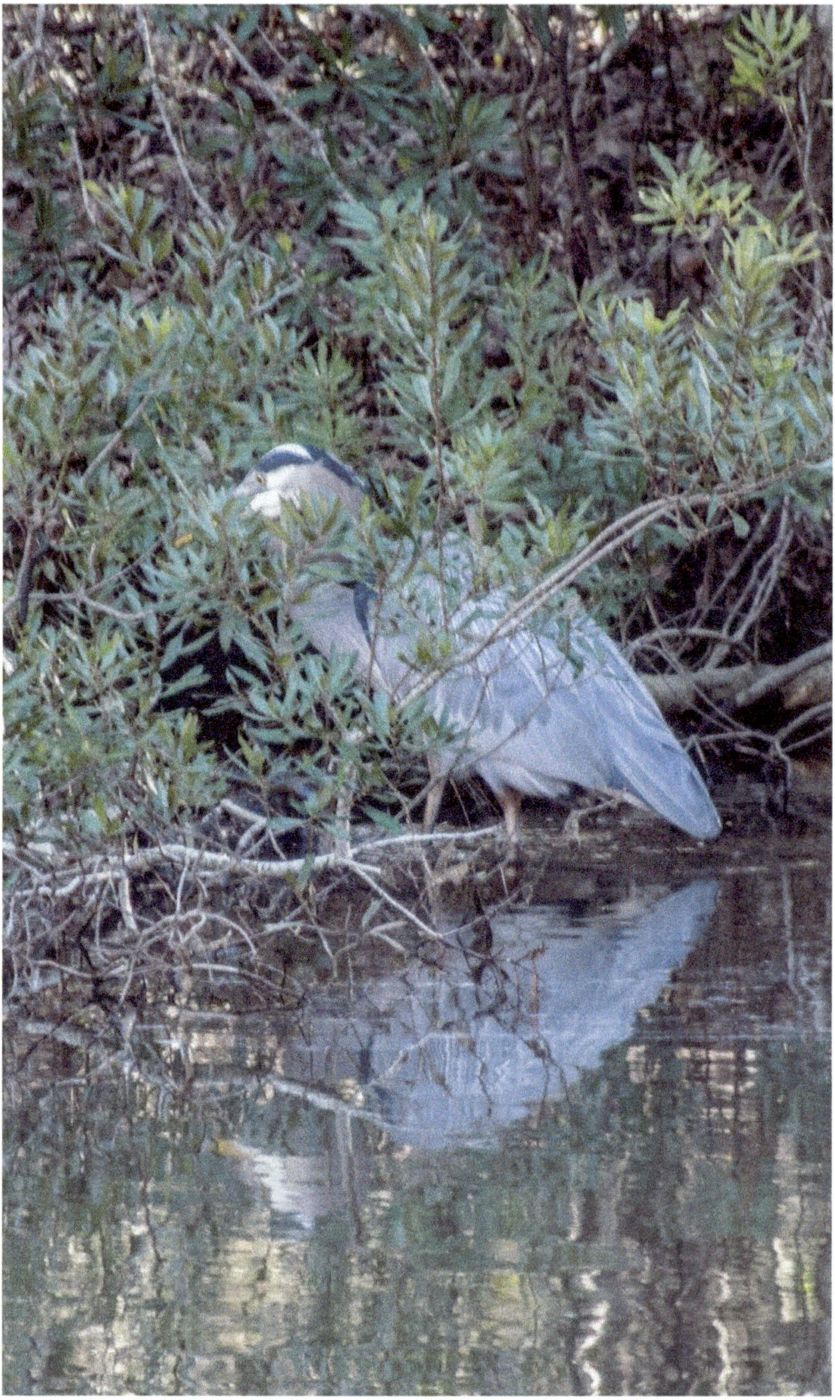

Time allows us to recapture the moments taken. Re-assess the past and value the future with assurance.

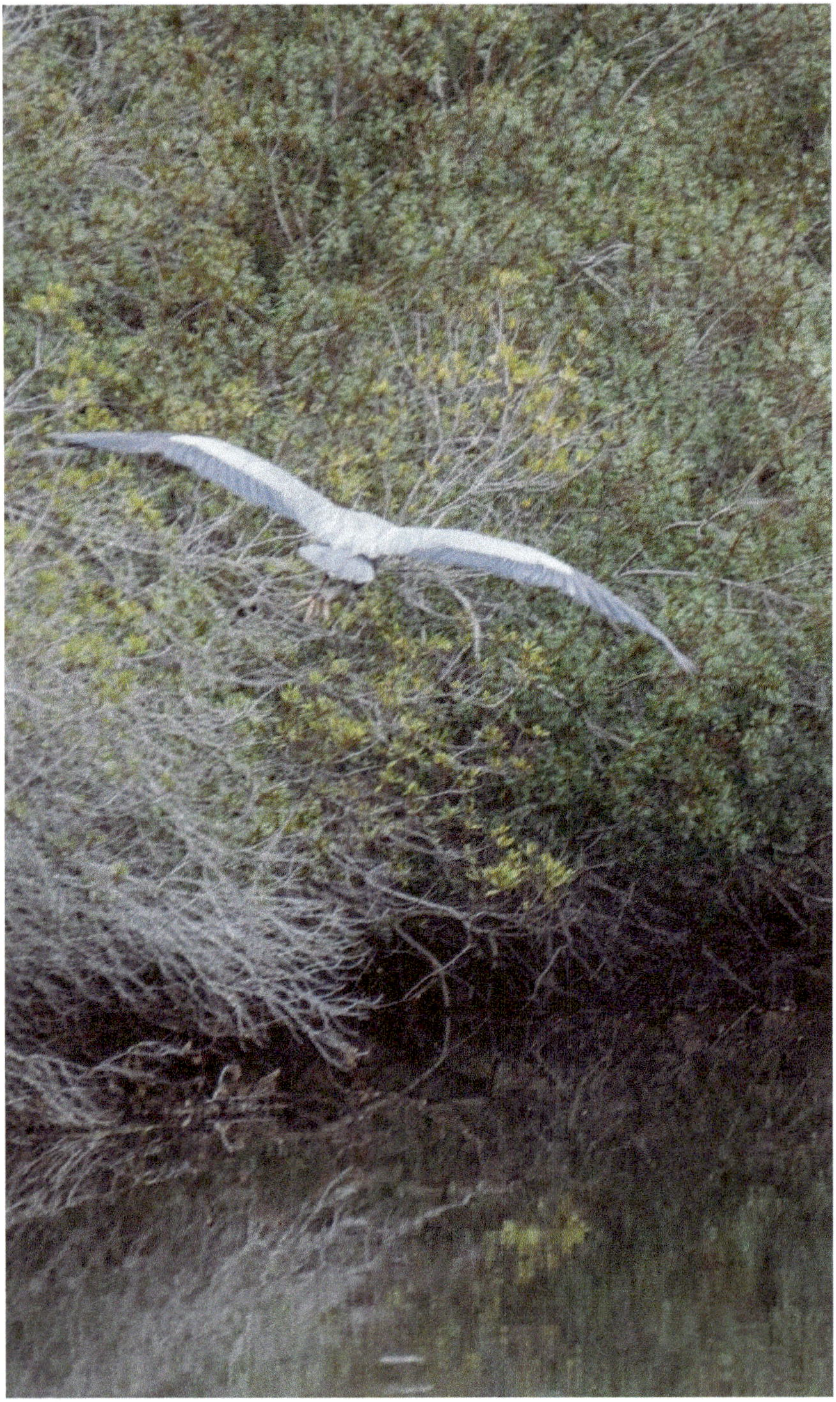

Wanting to stop, but never wanting the ride to end. Be one with your surroundings and make them boundless.

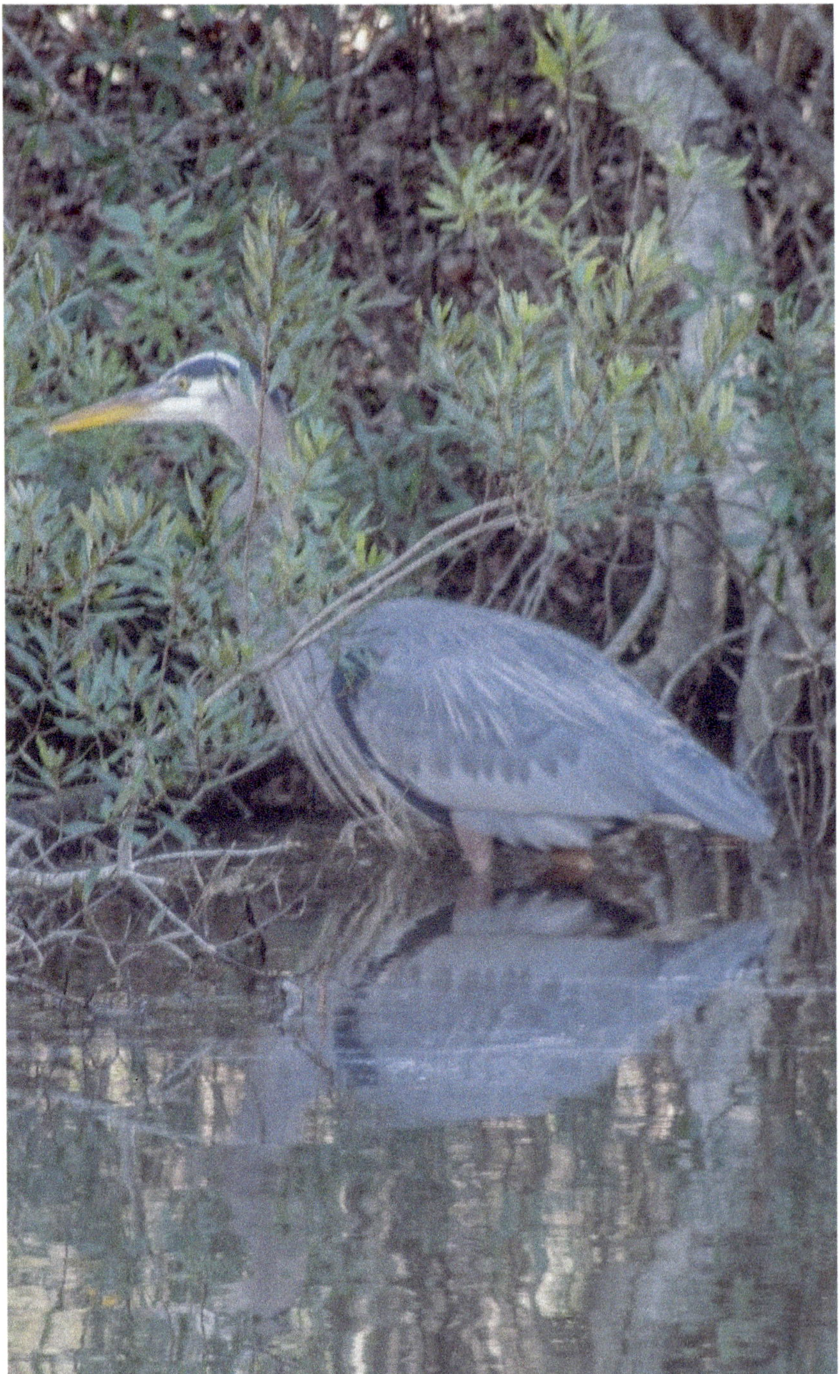

Never look back for the vast world awaits the presence of your being. Know the worth you bring forward as they await your essence.

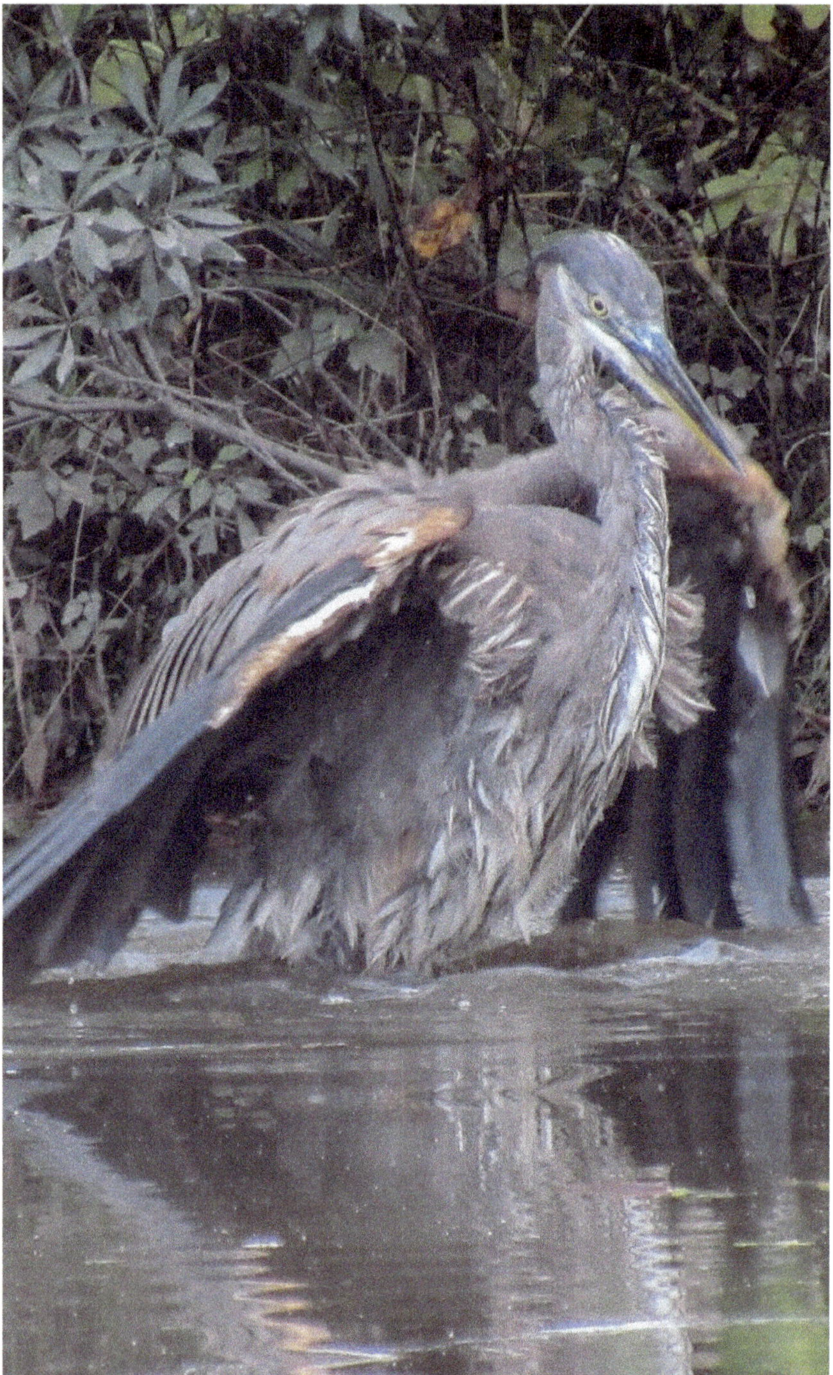

Looking back with curiosity and strength. Join us on the

road to life.

Learn to live and love, completely.

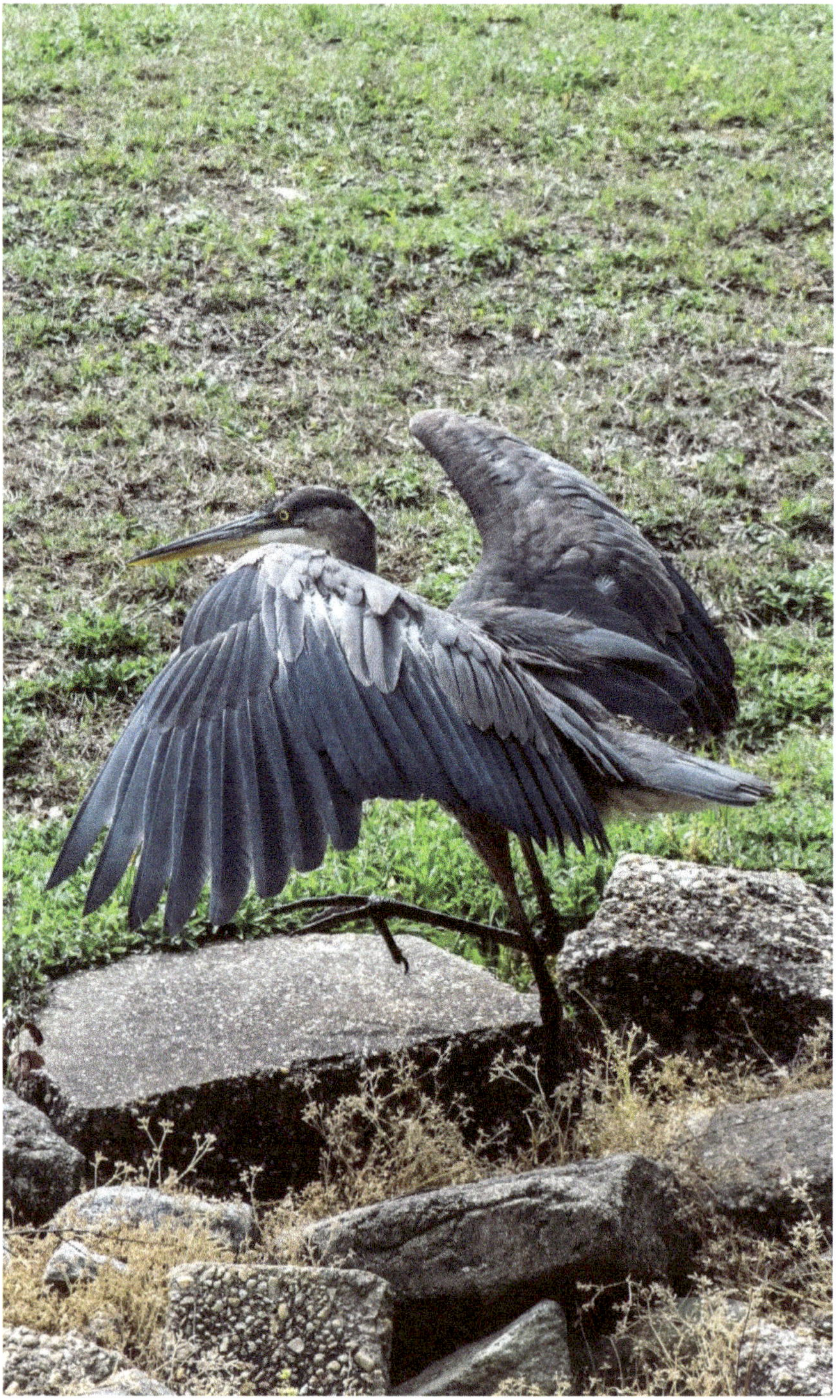

Our path is ongoing. No loss of identity. Being who you are impacts the magnificence of who you will become.

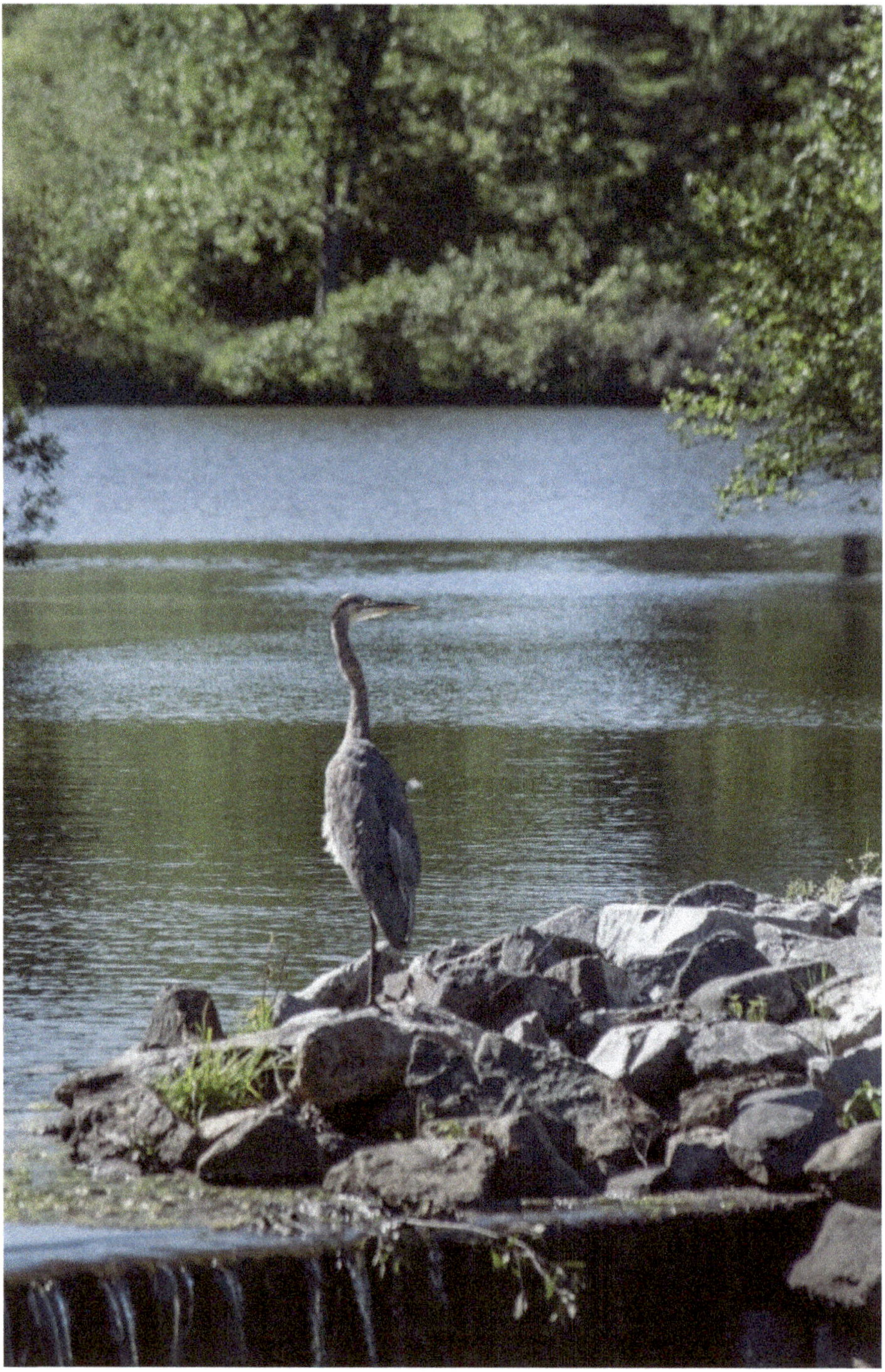

On the edge of a precipice, love abounds. Life is real and belongs to us, valued friend. Freedom is an empowered miracle. Enjoy.

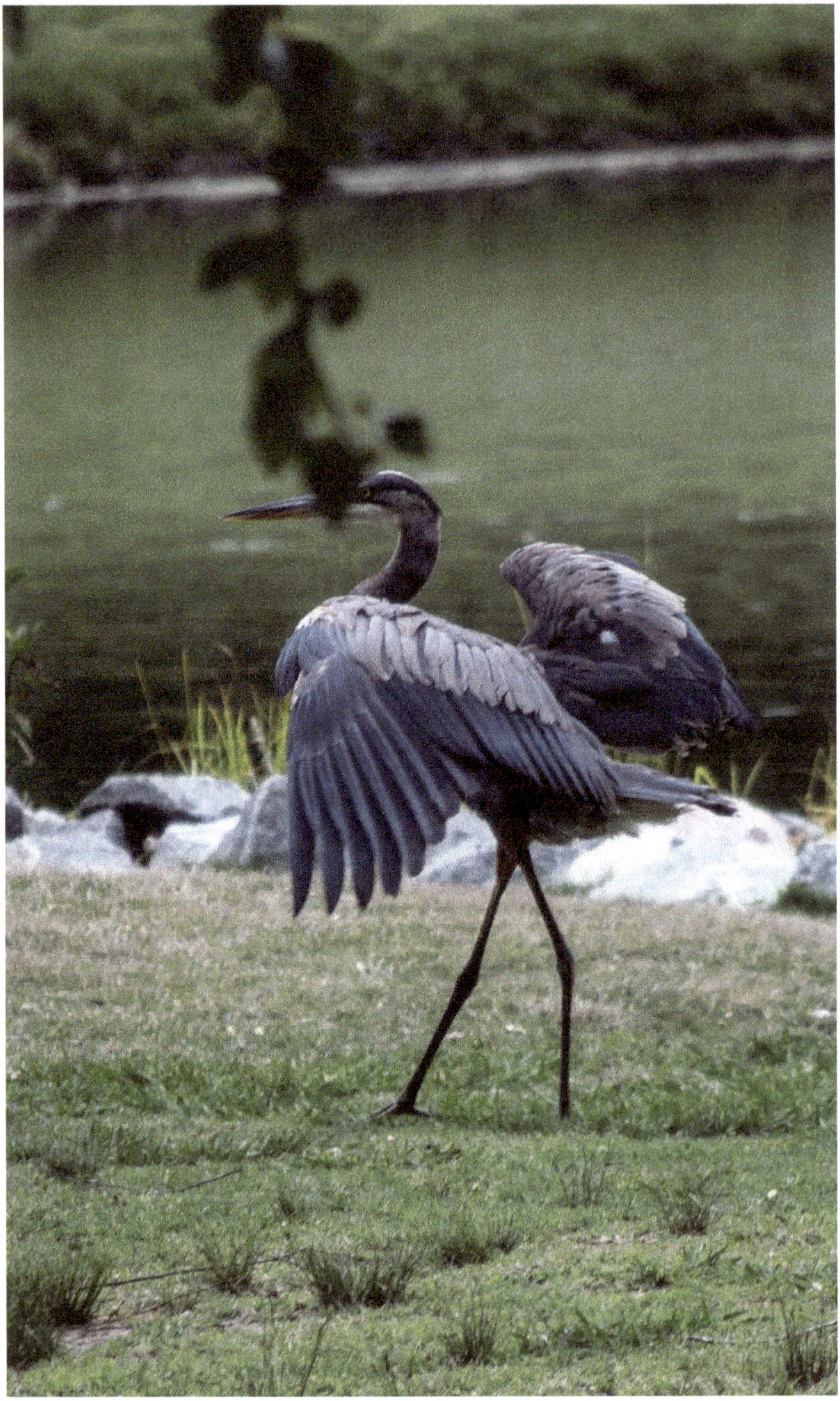

Our thoughts span a time unknown. Never consider the least you are capable of, but strive for the impact of making a welcome difference.

Dance like no one is watching.

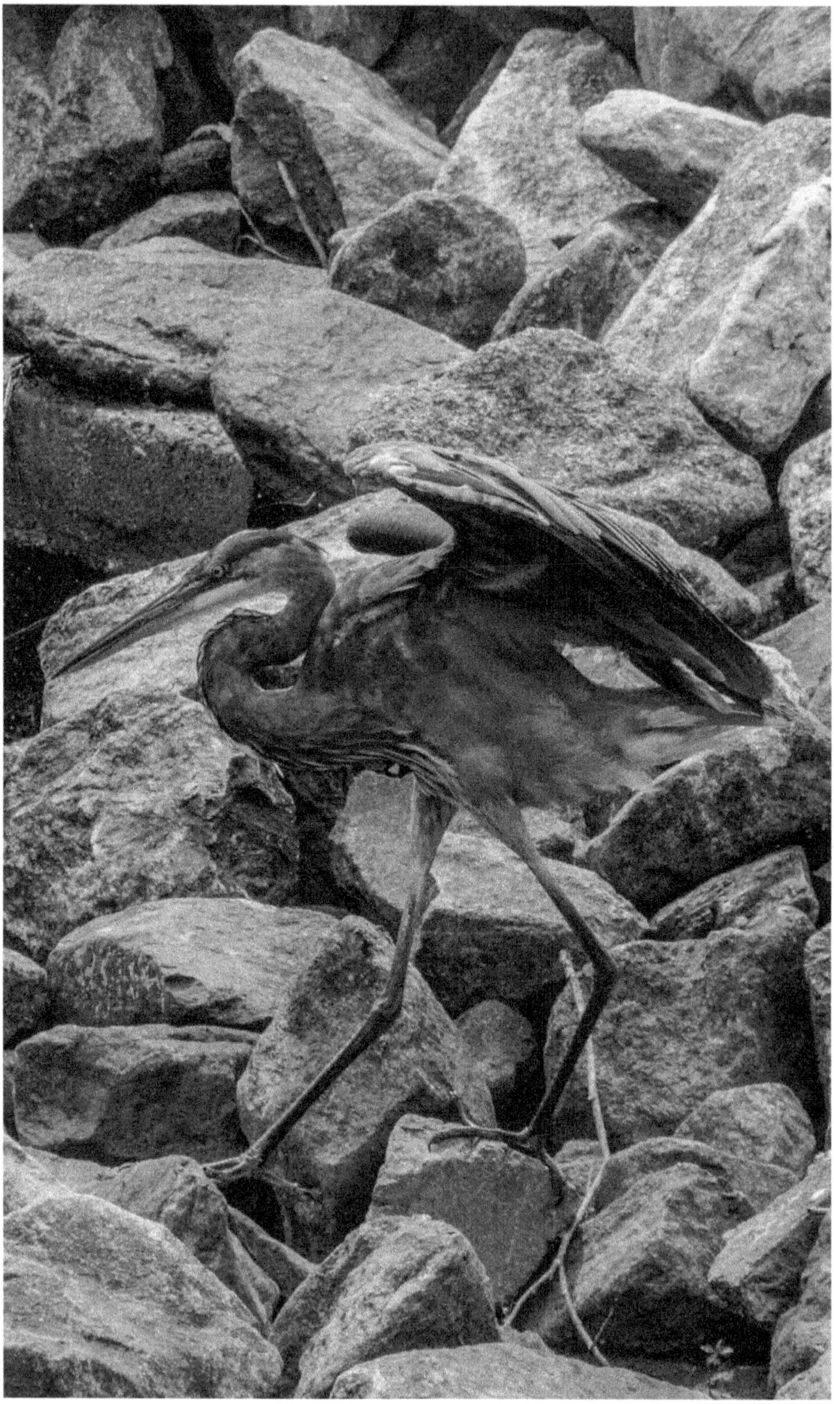

One stepping stone leads to the next. Be ready for the path ahead and explore the fullness of nature.

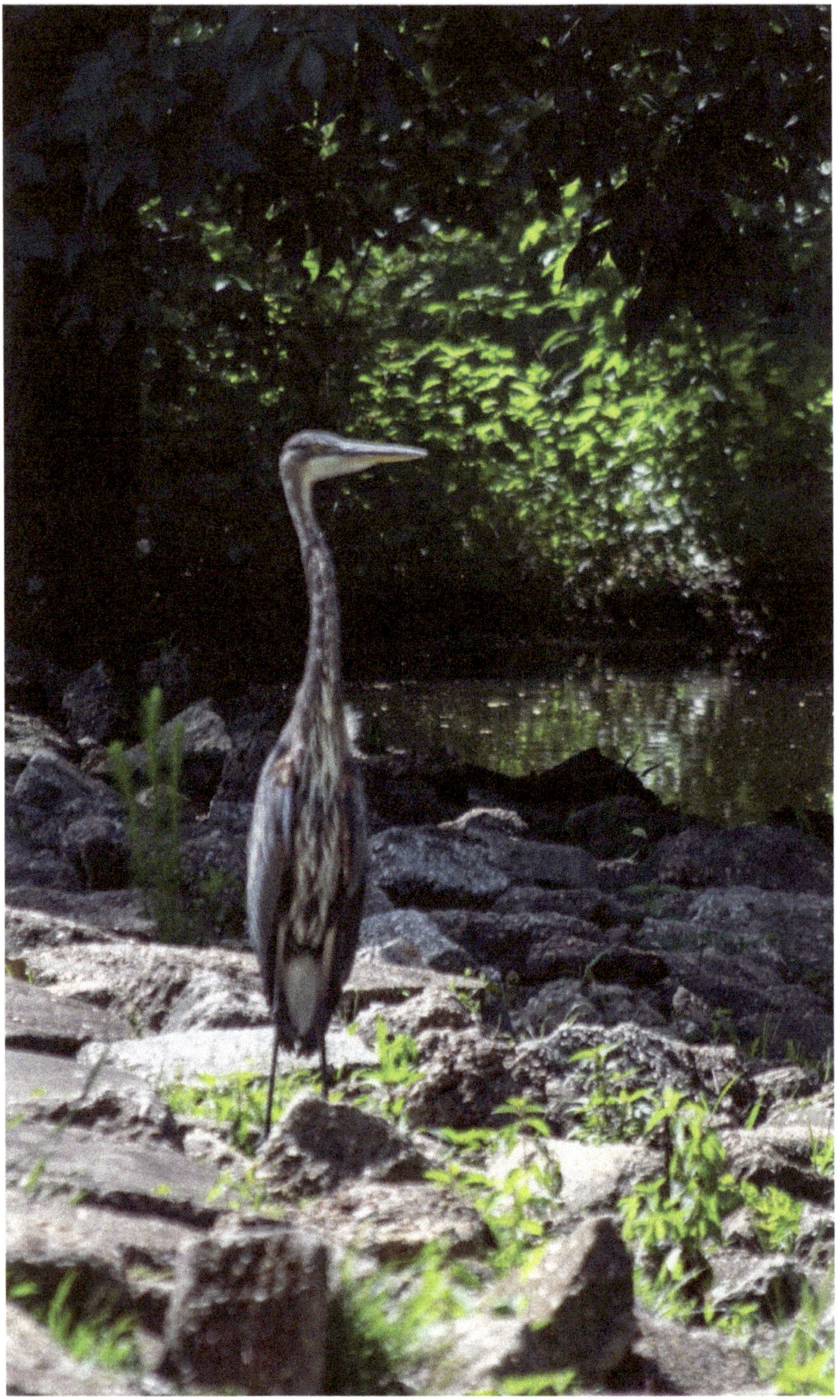

Stand ready to view the world anew. With determination and prowess, look far beyond the inevitable.

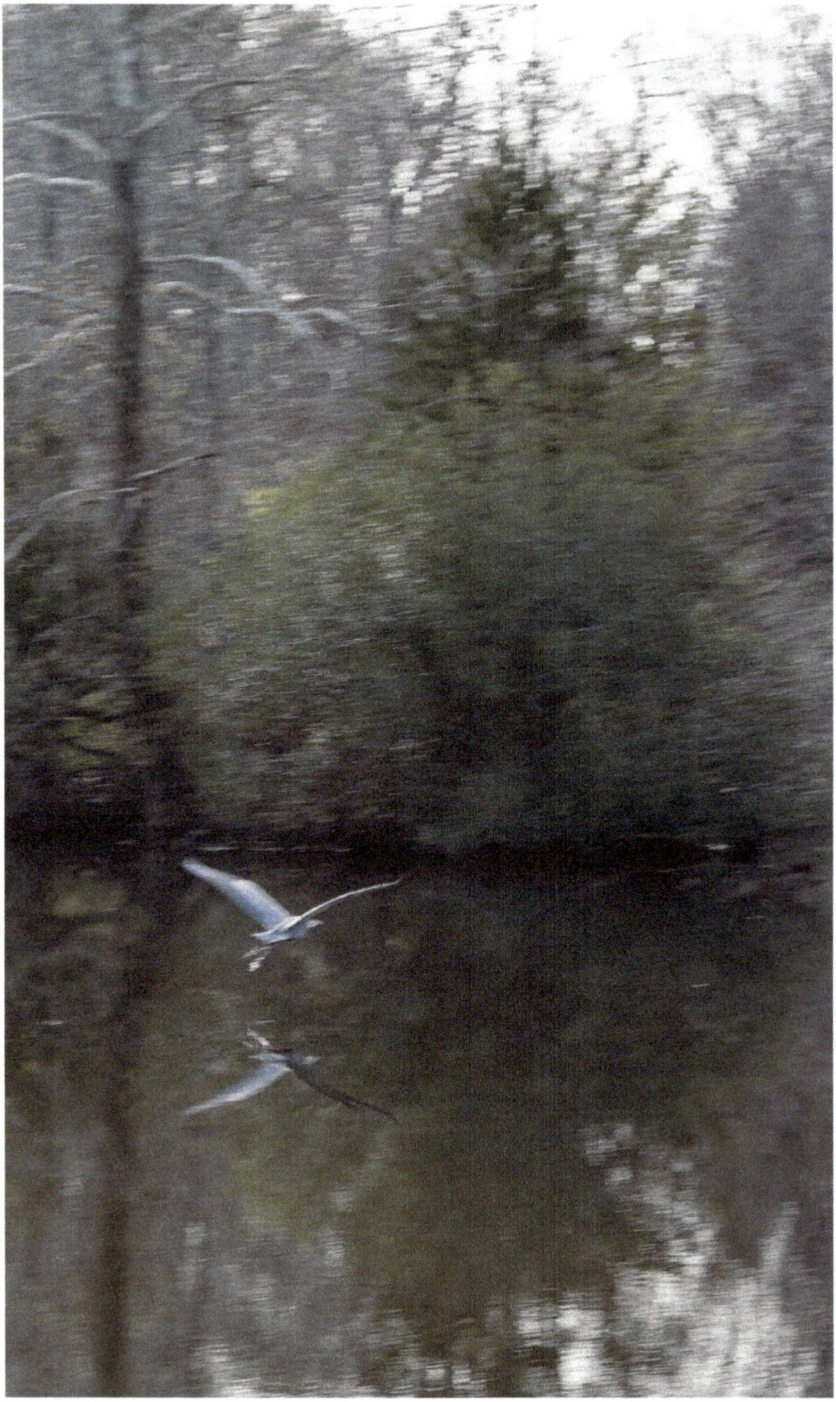

Feel the joy of being free. Lift your spirits to rival mine. We have no limits, simply a series of serendipitous chances to fulfill the greatness of life.

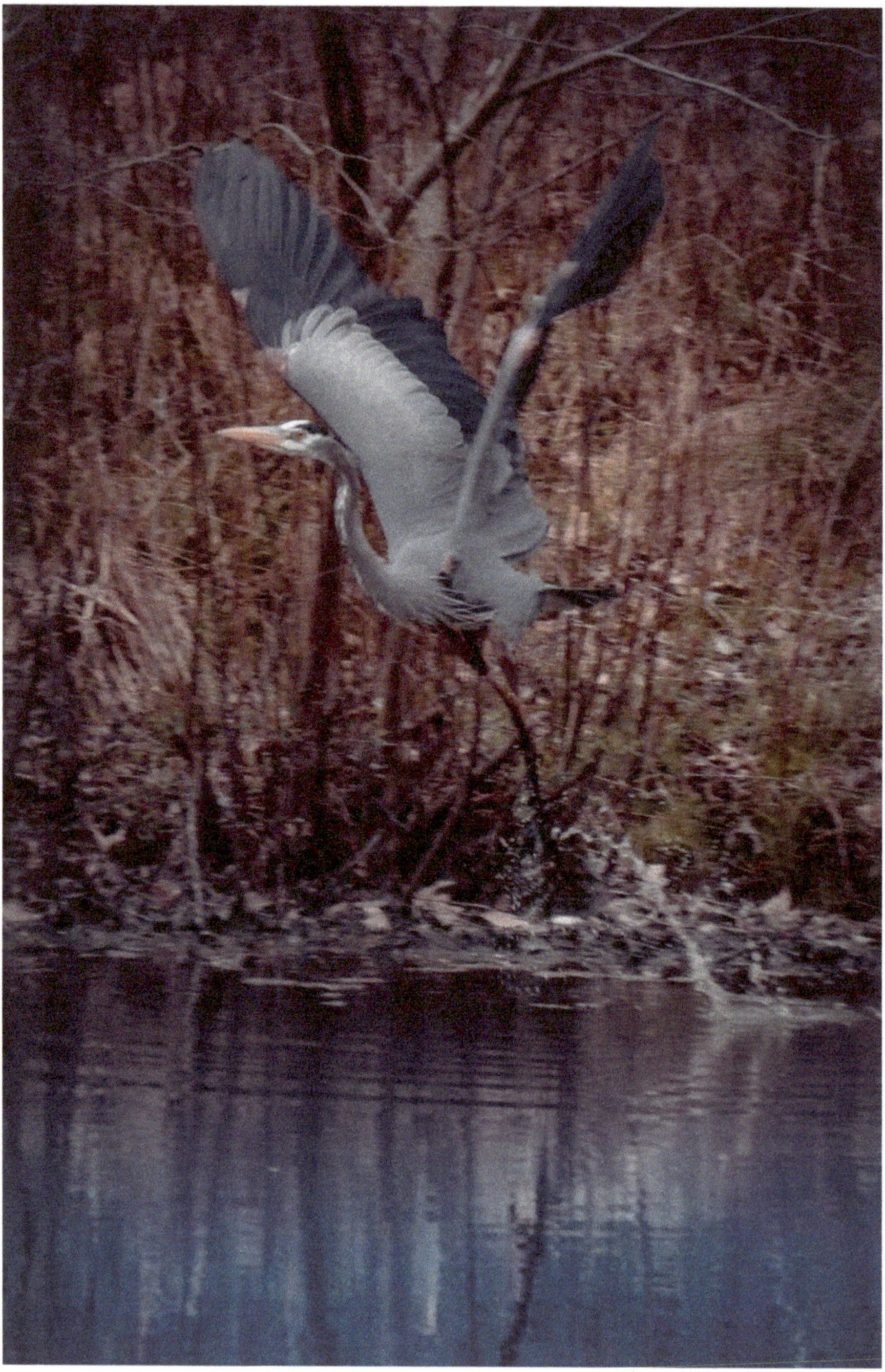

Perfectly angled for destiny to lead us afar. Never fearful, but always challenged by time. Face reality and make it better.

For that is enough.

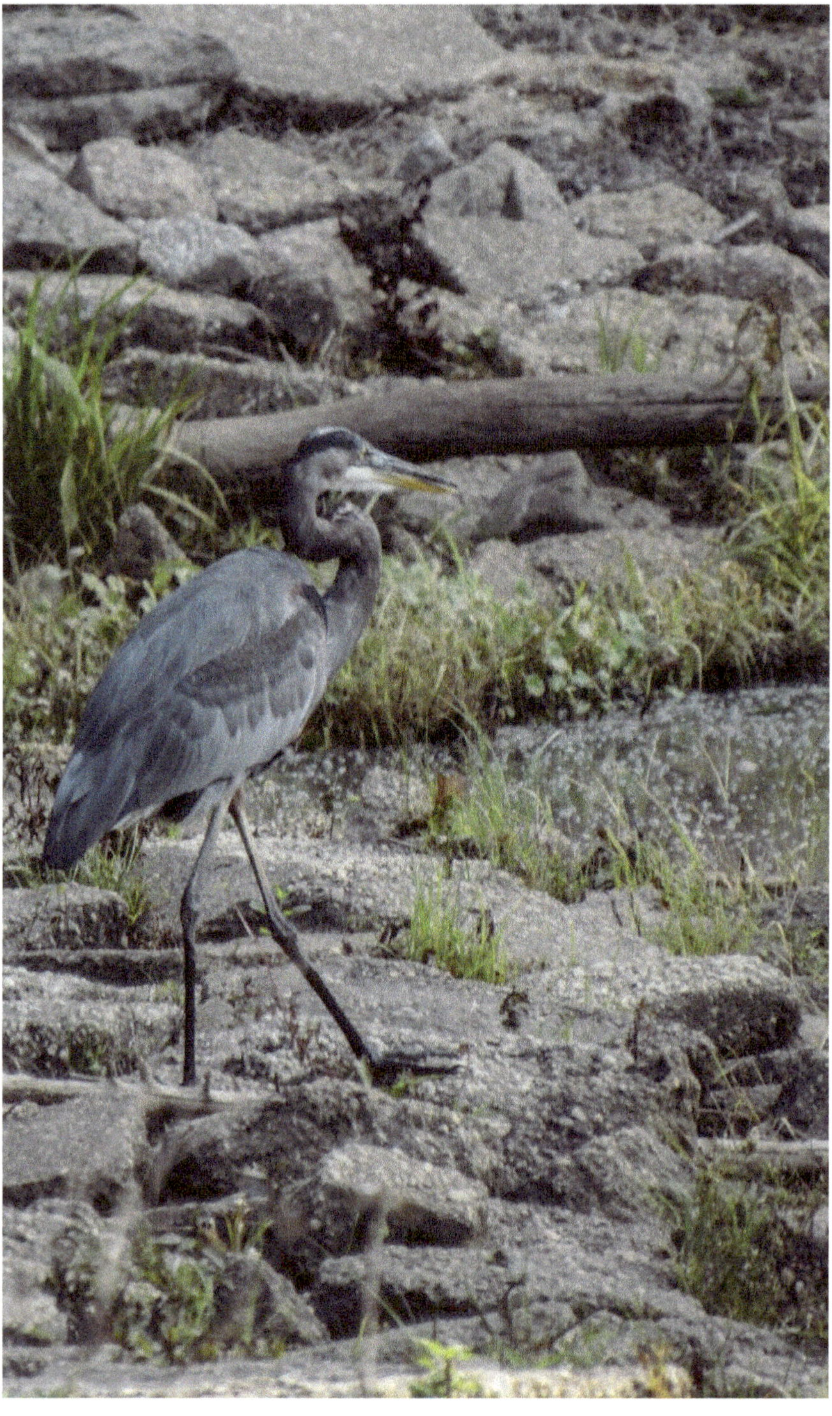

Confirm the energy felt deep within. Face the many challenges provided continuously. Be your best and make reality finer than expected.

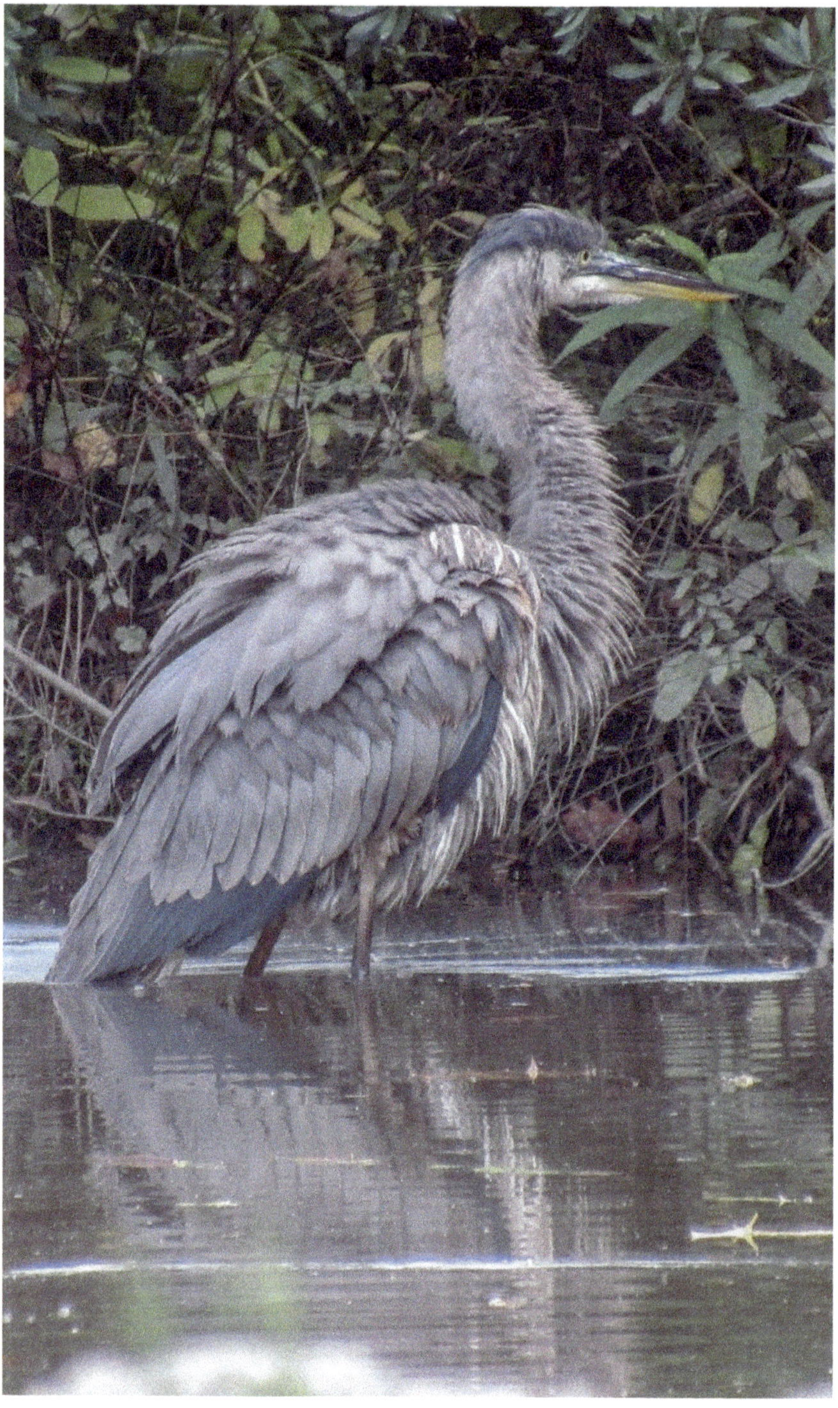

A majestic moment. The natural aura you bring to life

provides a serenity, a natural sparkle, and an inspiring

vision to a timeless existence.

Smooth your ruffled feathers and move ahead.

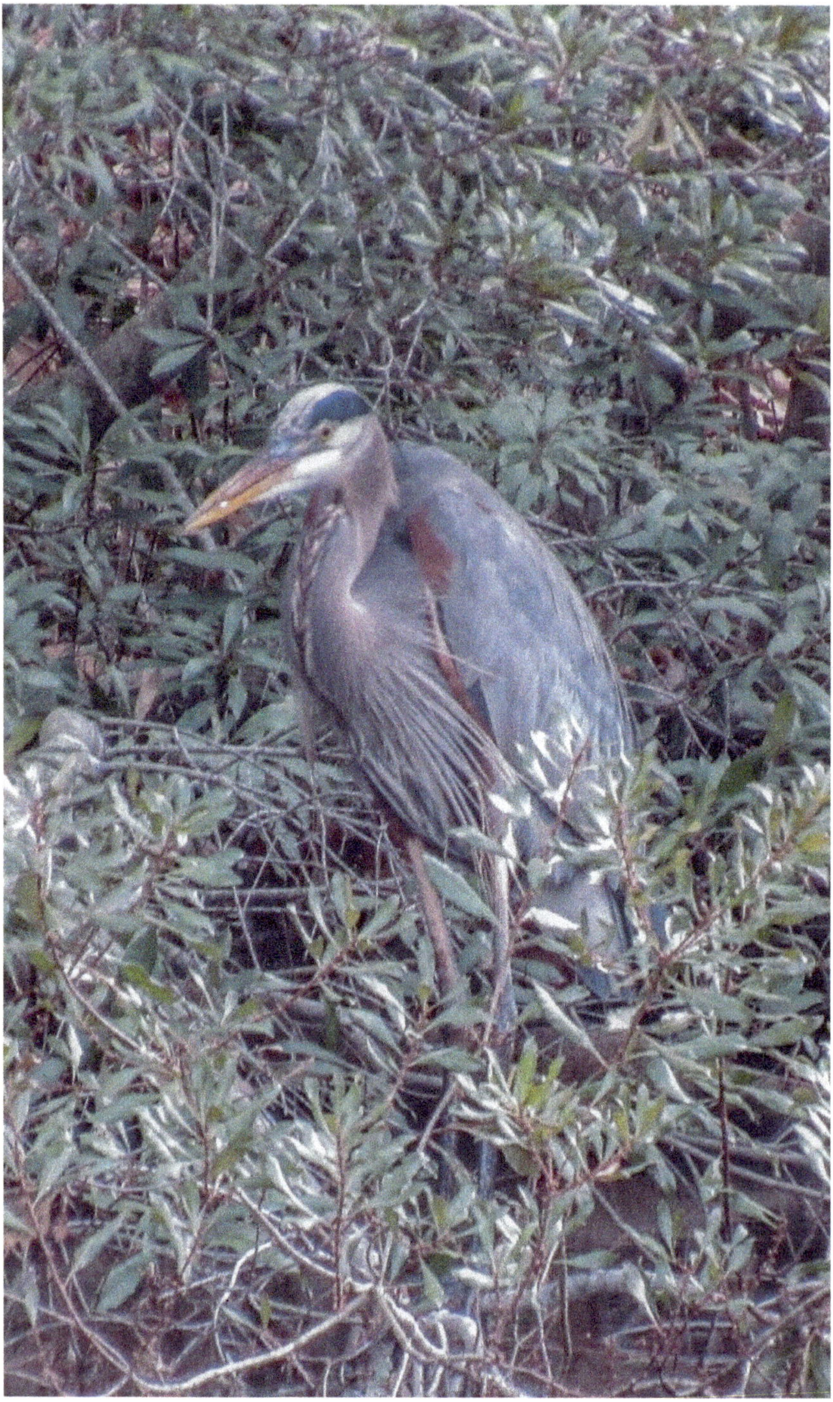

Beautiful Blue. The cycle of life continues for all.

Successful day with many more to follow.

Rejoice in the glory you bring to the world.

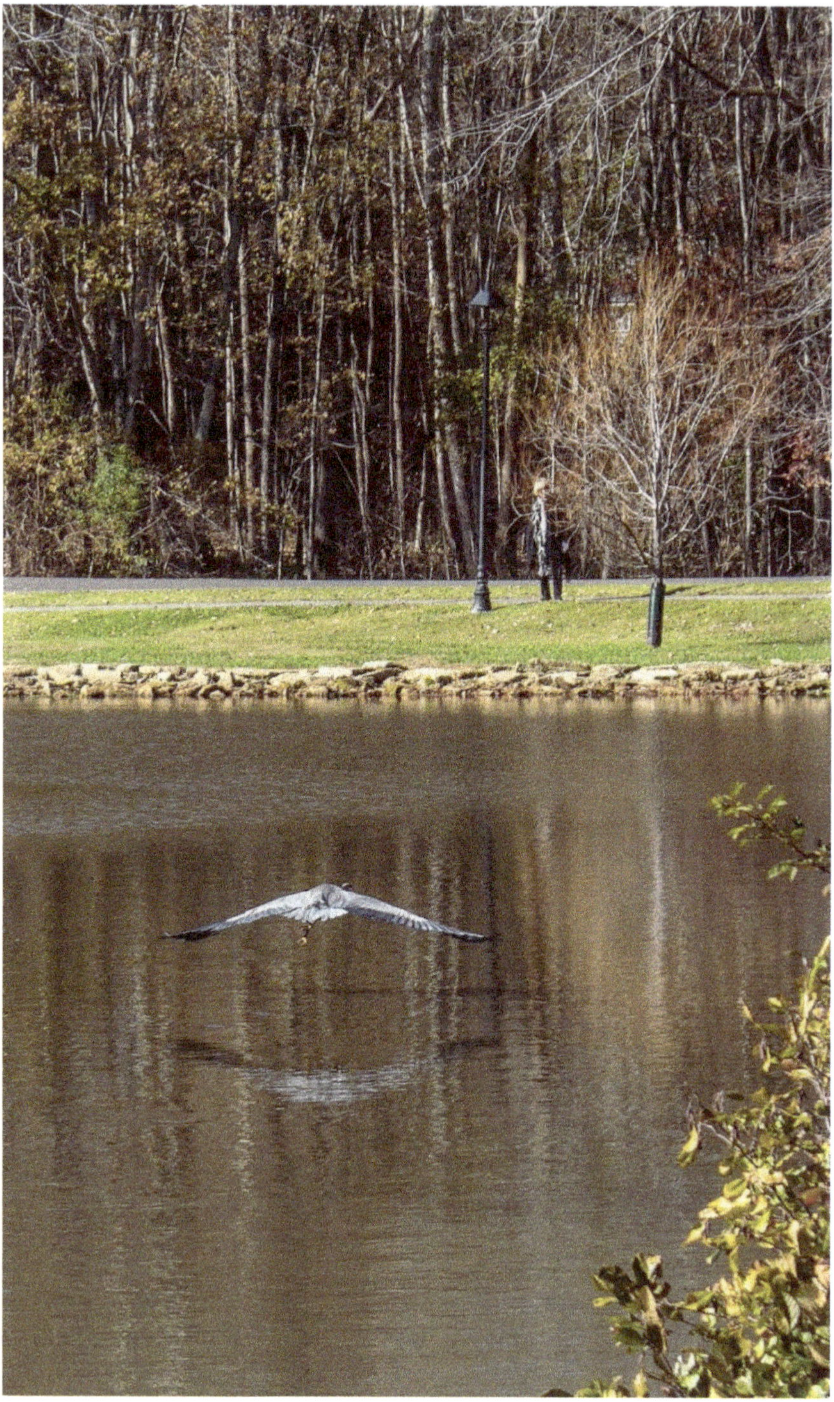

We see you, kind lady. Thank you for giving voice with

heartfelt sincerity and desire. Your words fill us with hope

for the future and beyond,

always.

About the Authors

Michael Richardson PE

Michael is a retired Professional Engineer with a career spanning service as an Army officer, an industrial engineering manager, a designer and builder of US Embassies and an operational test director for the Department of Homeland Security. Taking up photography in retirement, he captures the natural beauty of his home's environment as well as many of the images of life in Williamsburg, Virginia. A small pond near his home enticed a Blue Heron and many other water fowl to model for his benefit and for your enjoyment. The joy of sharing these images provides the motivation to record new experiences every day.

Michael co-authored BEAUTIFUL BLUE & YOU with his wife, Melinda, as their first series of nature/self-help books. His second book, BEAUTIFUL BLUE & YOU . . . TOO, reflects a continuing love of nature and relevance of changes that will enhance our growth and development throughout a lifetime.

Dr. Melinda Lincoln-Richardson

Melinda is an educator, teacher, and professor with advanced degrees in English, Speech, Drama, Professional Teaching Studies, Mediation, and a Doctoral of Arts Degree in Communication. Her first published book, Conflict Resolution Communication: Patterns Promoting Peaceful Schools, published by Rowman & Littlefield, presents a solid option for safe and peaceful schools. Challenging her creative abilities, she channeled her stream of consciousness and applied narrations to enhance the essence of each photo captured in BEAUTIFUL BLUE & YOU ... TOO. Melinda believes a joint collaboration with her husband is a gift to be shared with others.

Melinda co-authored BEAUTIFUL BLUE & YOU with her husband, Michael, as their first series of nature/self-help books. Her second book, BEAUTIFUL BLUE & YOU ... TOO, reflects a continuing love of nature and relevance of changes that will enhance our growth and development throughout a lifetime.

CPSIA information can be obtained
at www.ICGtesting.com
Printed in the USA
JSHW042018170723
44915JS00008B/45